Make a Grand Time of It

In the spirit of the Bards of old, Hugin the Bard tells the ancient stories of the *Mabinogion* through song, verse, and entertaining folktales—bringing the ancient tradition of the Bard into the present. Here is a rich and varied selection of songs celebrating the seasons, sabbats, and gods, interspersed with tidbits of magical knowledge and lore delivered by a real-life Bard.

Take a musical journey through the Celtic world and discover the adventure, romance, and poetry of the *Mabinogion*—ancient Welsh myths cleverly translated for the modern day by Hugin the Bard. Here are stories, legends, and anecdotes to accompany the songs and to enrich your life with the gift of insight and laughter. *A Bard's Book of Pagan Songs* will make rituals and celebrations fun and more rewarding.

Filled with nearly 60 original songs, *A Bard's Book of Pagan Songs* is an invaluable and thoroughly enjoyable resource for your next feast, festival or gathering. Each song is presented in condensed lead-sheets that include the key signature, chords and melody line of the first verse, plus the chorus of each song, lyrics, and chord charts. Everything you need to play or sing these songs is provided—even if you have only a basic familiarity with reading music, you'll be playing these tunes in no time, thanks to Hugin's expert guidance.

Dragon's Breath
Hollybush Studio
Fore Street, Tintagel
North Cornwall PL34 0DB
Telephone 01840 770050

About the Author

Hugin the Bard was born under the Sun sign of Leo in the year the English repealed their Witchcraft Laws (1951). His birthplace—Minneapolis, Minnesota—is a land with the full range of seasons, from frozen winters to scorching summers.

He was born to a large family, many of whom share the gifts of psychic ability to one degree or another. Some of his family members train, study, and worship together in the arts magickal.

Hugin has studied both Wiccan and Native American ways traditionally and informally. He has been a musician since 1963, sometimes performing professionally with the likes of Pete Seeger and Country Joe MacDonald. Hugin has always been ready to share his music with those wanting to hear it. On a Solstice, that may be a group of modern pagans, or a group of Native Americans at a pow-wow. At other times, his audience has been workers struggling for their rights on a picket line, inner-city youth trying to avoid the dangers of substance abuse, seniors caught in society's neglect, or just a small group of friends around the campfire.

A Marine Corps veteran of the Viet Nam War era, Hugin knows what it means to be a Peaceful Warrior or Warrior for Peace, which he is in heart and spirit.

To Write to the Author

If you wish to contact the author or would like more information about this book, please write to the author in care of Llewellyn Worldwide, and we will forward your request. Both the author and publisher appreciate hearing from you and learning of your enjoyment of this book. Llewellyn Worldwide cannot guarantee that every letter written to the author will be answered, but all will be forwarded. Please write to:

Hugin the Bard
℅ Llewellyn Worldwide
P.O. Box 64383-K603, St. Paul, MN 55164-0383, U.S.A.

Please enclose a self-addressed stamped envelope for reply, or $1.00 to cover costs.
If outside U.S.A., enclose international postal reply coupon.

Free Catalog from Llewellyn Worldwide

For more than 90 years, Llewellyn has brought its readers knowledge in the fields of metaphysics and human potential. Learn about the newest books in spiritual guidance, natural healing, astrology, occult philosophy, and more. Enjoy book reviews, new age articles, a calendar of events, plus current advertised products and services. To get your free copy of *Llewellyn's New Worlds of Mind and Spirit*, send your name and address to:

Llewellyn's New Worlds of Mind and Spirit
P.O. Box 64383-K603, St. Paul, MN 55164-0383, U.S.A.

A Bard's Book of Pagan Songs

Stories and Music from the Celtic World

Hugin the Bard

1996
Llewellyn Publications
St. Paul MN USA 55164-0383

A Bard's Book of Pagan Songs © 1996 by Hugin the Bard. All rights reserved. Printed in the United States of America. No part of this book may be used or reproduced in any manner whatsoever without written permission from Llewellyn Publications, except in the case of brief quotations embodied in critical articles and reviews.

FIRST EDITION
First Printing, 1996

Cover design: Anne Marie Garrison

ISBN 1-56718-603-3

Llewellyn Publications
A Division of Llewellyn Worldwide, Ltd.
P.O. Box 64383-K603 St. Paul, MN 55164-0383

Bardic Copyright

I declare before The Gods that I, Hugin The Bard, did write the songs, lyrics and arrangements set forth in this manuscript, except where duly noted.

Any who would share these songs with friends, coveners or other like kindred may rest assured they are complying with the wishes of the author and The Muse. If you would also share the origin of these songs, the ego of the author would be well fed. Included in this are performers whose income from the performance of these songs would be considered gratuitous or modest.

Those who would reproduce any of this material for profit are advised to consult Federal and International Copyright Laws and the publisher of this manuscript lest the weight of karmic retribution fall heavily upon all aspects of their lives.

So Mote It Be!

Dedication

This manuscript is dedicated to The Muse in all Her creative aspects.

Acknowledgements

Recognition must go out to my parents, grand-parents and other ancestors for making me who I am.

Within the Craft of the Wise, recognition goes out to Ladies Silverbow, Myfanwy, Amethyst, Emer, Shadow Cat, Susy Jeffrey and The Blue; also to Lords Stormbringer and Cu Chulain, Carl Weschcke of Llewellyn Publications and Brother Muninn.

Last, but certainly not least, an enormous amount of gratitude and recognition must go to Sheila Nunn, without whose help and support this manuscript might not exist.

By these words,

Hugin The Bard

Table of Contents

Page
- 1 What is a Bard? What was a Bard?
- 3 Lead Sheets
- 4 Some of the Music Symbols
- 5 The Mabinogion
- 7 (A Note On The Gaelic)
- 8 The Songs
- 9 <u>Bardic Tales From The Mabinogion</u>
  (Part I) <u>Tales of Olde Dyved</u>
- 10 Descent Into Annwn
- 15 Rhiannon Of The Birds
- 21 Child Named Grief
- 26 Island Of The Mighty
- 35 Caswallon's Quarry
- 39 Came A Storm
- 45 The Pigs of Pryderi
- 51 (Part II) <u>Children of Dôn</u>
- 55 On The Wind
- 59 The Dreams Of Arianrhod
- 63 A Very Funny Man
- 67 Lady, My Lady
- 71 Blodeuwedd
- 75 The Cauldron And The Goat
- 77 An Oak Grows
- 81 Cad Goddeu (Battle of The Trees)
     based on the translation by Robert Graves
- 90 <u>Feasting The Wheel</u>
- 93 The Wheel
- 97 Watch The Wheel Turn (Yule)
- 101 The King Shall Return (Imbolc)
- 105 Spring Fling (Vernal Equinox)

Page
109 Blooming of the Lady (Beltane)
113 On This Longest Day (Summer Solstice)
117 John Barleycorn (Traditional)
121 Stand Ye Up For A Boon (Lughnassad)
125 Autumn Again (Fall Equinox)
129 Dark Night (Hallows)
133 Drifting Through Time
139 The Dancers Band
143 Aye of Newt
145 Haul Away Home
149 Cosmick Cowboy
153 Northern Meadow
157 A Turtle Island Song
161 Wandering Minstrel
165 Love On The Astral Plane
169 Tarry On
173 The Fey, They Come
177 Since Last Time
181 The Messenger
185 Dance With Me Darlin
189 They Call Us Witches
193 Within The Well
195 Greenwood Down
199 Maidens and Wizards and Fools
203 Invocation
206 Blessed Be The Gods
209 Three Buckles
213 Feather In My Hand
217 Knights Of The Moon
221 Golden Embers
225 The Circle Goes Around

Page
228 Lady Of The Moon
231 The Mystery
235 Shenandoah (Traditional)
239 Reclaimed
240 Goddess Delight
243 Promise Me True
247 The Walrus And The Lizard
251 Balmy Spring Night
255 Muse of Mine
259 Departing Salutation

What is a Bard?

Since the time of William Shakespeare, Bard has been thought of as one who creates prodigiously in the literary or musical fields, especially poetry.

What was a Bard?

A Bard used to be one whom we would today think of primarily as a performing musician. The main distinction between a Bard and a minstrel, or other musician, was in the content of the material sung about. The peoples' history, mythology, cosmology and spiritual perspective were the primary subject matter of a Bards' trade. They told long tales in alliterative form at that time. Transmitted orally, the bardic tales were not written down until about the fourth or fifth century of the common era.

A Bard was also an initiated member of the priesthood. As such, they were highly trained in magick, ritual, music, language, the stars, healing and sometimes in the arts of combat.

   Always respected and sometimes feared, the Bard would receive food and lodging wherever they went. In exchange, the host would be entertained and hear news from the places the Bard had travelled.

   More than just an entertainer, a Bard was a spiritual teacher and healer who would travel the strands of the web of the people cementing the bonds wherever they may be.

Lead Sheets

    The sheets of music in this book are not in full manuscript form. They are in a condensed form known as "lead sheets". That is lead, as in "follow the leader". Lead sheets portray the key signature, chords and melody line of the first verse and chorus of each song. Not portrayed in lead sheets are musical introductions, harmony notes, passages between verses and choruses, melody and phrasing for later verses and song endings. These omitted items are, usually, best left to the interpretation of the performer.

    The sequencing of verse and chorus are to be found on the pages following the lead sheets where each songs' complete lyrics are given. Whenever possible, I have also given chord charts marked off by measure. Once the basic melody is known, the song may be played using the lyrics and chord charts on those pages following the lead sheets.

Some of the Music Symbols

- Ⓥ A circle with a "v" or a number inside marks the beginning of a verse.

- ⊡ A "c" inside a square box marks the beginning of a chorus.

- △ A "B" inside a triangle marks the beginning of a musical bridge when a third musical passage is used.

- ⊙ Cadenza is also called "the old eagle eye" by some jazz musicians. Found above the musical staff, it instructs to hold the note beneath it for a length of time to be determined by the performer.

- D△ A small raised triangle after a chord letter designates it as a major seventh chord.

- G/F# The first letter is the chord. The letter following the slash is the bass note to be played with it.

The Mabinogion

The book commonly known as The Mabinogion is a collection of ancient Welsh tales, rich in adventure, romance and poetry. The tales have been told, retold and translated many times. Each time, the storyteller or literary scholar makes minor changes or embellishments, molding the tales to a slightly better fit within their own mind and times.

Lady Charlotte Guest deleted some passages in her classic 1849 translation which she thought "indelicate". Medieval Christian scribes, certainly, changed parts of the older tales which came from pagan times. I have adapted, from several versions, the stories as I choose to tell them.

It is difficult to accurately trace the history of tales originating from an oral tradition prior to the common use of written records. Our primary medieval sources are The White Book of Rhydderch, The Red Book of Hergest and a manuscript referred to as Peniardd Six, all from about the 13th century. Charles Squire alludes to an earlier manuscript of 6th century poems, but it is doubtful such a manuscript still exists.

Medieval scribes added several romances which are not greatly different in style from the romances being written at about the same time in France. They also added two stories which included King Arthur as a secondary character. However, this text is mainly concerned with those older tales known as The Four Branches of The Mabinogion.

A common style and interrelated characters thread through the four branches. They contain much of the myths and magick of the ancient peoples of Gwynedd in the north of Wales and of Dyved in the south.

In the spirit of the Bards of olde, I present my musical version of The Four Branches of The Mabinogion, traditionally known as 1. Pwyll, Lord of Dyved.
    2. Branwen, Daughter of Llyr.
    3. Manawyddan, Son of Llyr.
    4. Math, Son of Mathonwy.

(A Note On The Gaelic)

Modern spellings of the old Gaelic language vary considerably according to the translator. Pronounciation may also vary from place to place with regional accents. Much of the translated Gaelic matches our current English alphabet. There are a few important differences.

ƒ ~ Usually sounds like a "v".

ƒƒ ~ Like "f" as in feather.

ðð ~ Like "th" as in then.

th ~ As in thistle.

g ~ As in go, never like gem.

ll ~ With an aspirant preceding the "l" sound. Usually an "h", but sometimes a "ch" as in the German name Bach. Depends on one's accent.

c ~ Always "k" as in cane, never "s".

s ~ Always "s", never "z".

w ~ Like a long "u" as in true or soon.

y ~ Like a short "i" as in thin.

The Songs

Bardic Tales From The Mabinogion

(Part I)
Tales of Olde Dyved

Descent Into Annwn

Pwyll was Lord of Dyved at the time and he wished to go hunting in Glynn Cuch. Very early one morning, the hunting party set out. During the hunt, Pwyll and his hounds were separated from the main party. Deep within the forest, he saw a stag brought down by another pack of hounds. These dogs were all pure white with red eyes and ears.

He set his dogs upon the others to take the stag for himself. The white hounds retreated without resistance. Then a rider in gray approached on a gray horse and spoke of the rudeness and discourtesy of Pwyll to take the stag of another's kill.

"If I have done wrong, I will earn your friendship.", replied Pwyll. And so began Pwyll's journey to the western underworld called Annwn. For the Gray Man was none other than it's Lord, Arawn.

To earn that friendship, Pwyll must slay Havgan (Summer White), Lord of the eastern underworld who had long been trying to invade Arawn's realm. Rumors of Havgan's atrocities and mutilations upon the dwellers of Annwn had reached even the mortal realm of Dyved. To aid in the task, Arawn cast a spell so they would each take the likeness of the other and each would rule in the other's place til the task was done.

Pwyll was told that Havgan must be

killed by a single blow. At the time, it was considered the honorable thing to deliver a mercy stroke through the heart of a mortally wounded foe to shorten his suffering. However, it affected Havgan's magick so that he would jump up ready to fight again strong as ever on the morrow if shown mercy. This had been what prevented Arawn from defeating Havgan by himself.

    The disguises were effective and none in either realm knew it was not their own Lord in residence. Modron, Lady of Annwn, was saddened when the man she thought was her husband refused her advances in bed. Pwyll's refusal of her was an act of friendship and the defeat of his own carnal temptation. It was to prove beneficial to the land of Dyved for the rest of Pwyll's life.

    Some say the battle with Havgan consisted of a single blow by Pwyll. Others insist it was a tremendous combat which lasted all day. Suffice to say that Pwyll won by not delivering the mercy blow. Arawn and Pwyll then returned to their own realms and thereafter remained good friends.

Descent Into Annwn

words and music by Hugin The Bard

12

Descent Into Annwn

① My Lord he went a' hunting once before the break of day
　The hounds and he got parted from the men along the way
　And deep within the forest, the hounds were heard to bay
　Mighty Pwyll descended into Annwn

② There he met the western Lord of Death, the Man in Gray
　A mortal man he needed in an underworld fray
　The eastern Lord of Death is the one that Pwyll must slay
　Mighty Pwyll descended into Annwn

③ The eastern Lord was greedy, the West he wished to rule
　In order to defeat him, both kingdoms they must fool
　So, Pwyll would look like Arawn and he would look like Pwyll
　Mighty Pwyll descended into Annwn

④ He went upon his journey and he came upon a well
　Her golden light and healing waters cast a lovely spell
　But, Rhiannon and Pwyll's another story yet to tell
　Mighty Pwyll descended into Annwn

⑤ In Arawn's castle, no one was the wise
　The Queen was fair beyond compare, desire burned inside
　But, Pwyll was sworn to friendship, wouldn't lay between her thighs
　Mighty Pwyll descended into Annwn

⑥ Havgan met him at the ford, he seemed a golden youth
　That he would sever women's breasts, it didn't seem the truth
　Yet, slay him without mercy was the task ahead of Pwyll
　Mighty Pwyll descended into Annwn

⑦ The warriors clashed together, Havgan proved a mighty foe
Throughout the day, until the eve, his powers seemed to grow
Yet, Havgan fell in battle to a single mighty blow
Mighty Pwyll descended into Annwn

⑧ My Lord he went a'hunting once before the break of day
The hounds and he got parted from the men along the way
And deep within the forest, the hounds were heard to bay
Mighty Pwyll descended into Annwn

Descent Into Annwn
6/8 TIME
Ⓥ Verse

Dm	F	C	Dm
F	C	Dm	A
Dm	F	C	A
Dm	C	Dm	Dm
Dm	C	Dm	Dm

Rhiannon Of The Birds

In the land of Dyved is an ancient and man-made mound at Arberth where a great many magickal things have taken place. It is called Gorsedd Arberth (The Mound of Arberth). Whenever a Lord of Dyved should sit upon the mound, it is said he will either suffer wounds and blows or see a wonder.

Pwyll once chose to sit up there with trusted companions. That day they saw a beautiful woman in a bright golden gown ride by. Though her white horse travelled at a leisurely pace, she could not be approached. The faster a footman or rider did pursue her, the more did she outdistance them. All the while, she and her horse remained at their leisurely pace.

Finally, after Pwyll had driven his fastest horse in her pursuit til it could take no more, did he cry out to her, "O, Lady! For the sake of whom you most love, do wait for me!"

"I will gladly," said she, "And it were better for your horse had you asked sooner, for I have come to see you."

Her name was Rhiannon, daughter of Heveydd the Old. He would give her in marriage to one she did not love. She would marry him only if Pwyll rejected her, for she did love Pwyll. The Lord of Dyved was filled with joy and readily agreed to marry her, for he found that he cherished her above all others.

In a year and a day did Pwyll and ninety-nine companions follow Rhiannon's directions of how and when to cross the Bridge of Rainbows and thereby enter the land in which Rhiannon lived. It was a land whose dwellers had evolved to a higher degree than is known on mortal Earth. A land where violence and suffering and even death by old age were no longer known. The wedding hall was spectacular to the men of Dyved. The feast, wine and ale surpassed any they had known.

During the feast, a handsome young man came up to Pwyll and asked to be granted a boon. Being in good spirits, Pwyll replied, "Whatever you ask, if it is in my power to grant, you shall have." The man was Gwawl, to whom Rhiannon would have been wed by her father's wishes. Pwyll's speaking without thinking had just given away his new bride, for the boon he wanted was to be the groom at Rhiannon's wedding.

In those days, one's word was worth much more than it is today. So, the men of Dyved returned home quite disappointed. Still, Rhiannon had a plan.

In another year and a day, Pwyll and the ninety-nine returned, this time to the wedding feast of Rhiannon and Gwawl. While the men waited outside, Pwyll entered wearing rags and carrying a bag he'd been given by Rhiannon. The hall silenced when Pwyll requested a boon.

"I am not so foolish as you." said Gwawl, "If your boon be reasonable, I shall grant it."

"Just food," said Pwyll, "Enough to fill my little bag here."

Gwawl acceded to the boon and servants rushed to fill the small bag with food. But, no matter how much food went into the bag, it still looked nearly empty to the amazed assembly.

"This bag will only be filled when a man of noble birth steps into it with both feet and declares it full." cries Pwyll. At which, the frustrated Gwawl leaped into it with both feet. The bag then magickally extended up and over his head and was securely fastened by Pwyll.

One by one, the men of Dyved entered the hall, approached the bag and said, "What is this? It must be a Badger in the Bag!" and either kicked the bag or struck it with a stick. This is the earliest recorded playing of that game.

Gwawl was made to relinquish Rhiannon and promise to seek no revenge in order to be released. Rhiannon and Pwyll then completed their wedding feast and went together to rule in Dyved bonded by their love.

The price was actually quite high. For, they had visited both violence and suffering to that lofty land and in order for Rhiannon to enter Dyved, she must once again become as a mortal woman. She must once again know all the joys and discomforts of mortal life, even to age and then once again to die.

17

Rhiannon Of The Birds

words and music by Hugin The Bard

Rhiannon Of The Birds

1) Rhiannon of the Birds
    Beyond the Bridge of Rainbows
A land of beauty so fair
    That mortals would dare not compare
The castle had crystalline walls
    With roofing of birds o'er the halls

2) Rhiannon of the Birds
    Daughter of Dyved's first and ancient King
He would give her away
    To the best friend of death, their Lord Gray
Would rather give her to Gwawl
    Than see her be mortal with Pwyll

3) Rhiannon of the Birds
    She led her man to her bright world
At their wedding feast, Pwyll
    Behaved like a mortal fool
Tricked a moment too soon
    He gave her to Gwawl as a boon

4) Rhiannon of the Birds
    Wished to be wed to her mortal
Brought him back in a year and a day
    She told him just what to say
In a bag that would not be filled
    They broke Gwawl's suffering will

⑤ Rhiannon of the Birds
   Lover of the ancient harmonies
She went to Dyved as Queen
   The fairest they had ever seen
She went as a mortal to rule
   As mortal as her lover Pwyll

⑥ Rhiannon of the Birds
   Fairest daughter of Modron
She so loved a man
   That she gave up her heavenly land
To live life again as a mortal
   To grow old, to suffer and die

Rhiannon of the Birds

Rhiannon Of The Birds
4/4 TIME

Ⓥ Verse

| Dm | G | Am7 | F | Dm7 | G |

| C△ | F△ | C△ | F△ |

| Em7 | Am7 | Dm7 | G |

| C△ | F△ | C△ | F△ |

| Em7 | Am7 | Dm7 | G | G |

Child Named Grief

Rhiannon gave birth to only one child we know of, a son named Pryderi, which means anxiety or grief.

After a few years without an heir from Rhiannon and Pwyll, the Druids of Dyved wanted either a child from Rhiannon or for Pwyll to take another wife. A year and a day after their ultimatum, Pryderi was born. His paternity is somewhat in doubt.

Some believe his true father was Manawyddan, brother of the High King of Britain, who impregnated Rhiannon while in the magickal guise of Pwyll with Pwyll's consent. This would be a bit like the fabled origins of King Arthur. But, unlike the ambitious Uther who sired Arthur, Manawyddan had no desires of being King. Perhaps Pwyll had become sterile from his many trips away from the mortal plane.

The night after his birth, Pryderi was abducted by an other-worldly source. The women watching after mother and child, somehow, all fell asleep and woke to find the baby gone. They then killed a puppy, smeared the blood and bones on Rhiannon and claimed she had eaten the child.

For that alleged crime, the Druids sentenced Rhiannon to sit each day for seven years at the horse-block telling strangers and guests of the crime and to carry them into court on her back. But, few there were who would accept the ride.

(continues)

Child Named Grief

1. Young Pryderi, child named grief
    Your misbegotten woe
   Came from the hand of your mother's land
    From the friend of a jealous soul
   Pwyll is whom you'll call your father
    Though his seed had died
   Lord Manawyddan in Pwyll's guise
    Planted you inside

2. Stolen from your mother's side
    The night that you were born
   Found alone by Teyrnon
    Just before the morn
   Three colts lost, each on May Eve
    Teyrnon stood guard that night
   When he chopped off the monster's arm
    It dropped the babe so bright

3. Poor Rhiannon, framed for murder
    By her maids in waiting
   They claimed that she devoured him
    While they were a'sleeping
   Sentenced by enchanted Druids
    Seven years take heed
   She must carry on her back
    Court guests, and tell that deed

④ In the guise of minstrel
    Lord Manawyddan went
To show the warrior Teyrnon
    From where the babe was sent
When the lad was four years old
    He went home at last
To be again with Rhiannon
    Her long grief had passed

Child Named Grief
4/4 TIME

Ⓥ Verse

| G	| D	| C	| G |
| Am7	| D	| G	| D |
| G	| D	| C	| G |
| Am7	| D	| G	| G C G |
| Am7	| C	| G	| G |
| C	| Am	| D	| D |
| G	| D	| C	| G |
| Am7	| D	| G	| G C G |

(continued)

Meanwhile, in Gwent Below the Woods, Teyrnon ruled. It is said he was the best man in the world. Teyrnon had a mare which would foal every May Eve. But, each time the colt would be gone come morning. He stayed with the mare and colt one May Eve to watch and protect.

Late that night, a great claw reached into the stable seizing the colt. Teyrnon drew his sword and hacked the claw off at what seemed to be an elbow. The colt leaped free and Teyrnon pursued the withdrawing bloody stump of a limb. Outside the stable could be heard a great crash and a scream. He found only a newborn babe wrapped in a silk mantle. Teyrnon and his childless wife raised the boy as their own calling him Gwri Golden Hair.

Eventually, they heard of Rhiannon's plight and realized the child's origin. When the boy was returned to his true parents, Rhiannon exclaimed, "My grief is over." Thus was he renamed Pryderi by his mother.

Island Of The Mighty

(The tale of Branwen and the war called Morddwydtwyllyon)

  Matholuch, the High King of Ireland, sailed with men and ships to the Island of the Mighty seeking an alliance with Bran the Blessed, High King of all the island of Britain. He also sought the hand of Branwen of the White Breast, sister to Bran. Council was made and the two were agreeably wed amid a fine feast. Early the next morning, horses of the Irish King were discovered and mutilated by Evnissyen.

  Evnissyen was brother to Bran by their mother, Penardim. She was sister to Beli, the most recent High King. The paternity of her children was thus. Bran, Manawyddan and Branwen were sired by Llyr, her chosen mate. The twins, Nissyen and Evnissyen, came from a coerced mating with Euroswydd, who was later slain by Llyr for that coercion.

  The nature of the twins was opposite. Nissyen could make peace between hostile forces. Evnissyen could bring even the most loving brothers to quarrel. Because Evnissyen was of the royal family, his blood could not be shed to avenge his foul deed.

  To save the Irish King's honor, a face price of horses, a silver rod as tall as Matholuch, a golden plate and a sacred magickal cauldron were given to him. The Irish then returned home with their new Queen. Within a year, Branwen bore a son they named Gwern.

The royal succession of Britain at the time followed the custom of the old tribes, Mother-right. That is, the next King was born to the sister of the reigning King. Irish succession came by the Father-right custom of the new tribes. As such, Gwern could theoretically become King over both islands.

Remembrance of the harm done to Irish horses, sacred to the Irish Great Mother, festered til finally Branwen was punished for the deed. She was made to work in the cooking pit where each day the butcher would strike her ear as he finished his work. This went on for three years.

Branwen had rescued a wounded starling in the cooking pit. While nursing it to health, she taught it to speak. When it was fully recovered, the starling flew to Britain and told Bran of his sister's plight.

Now, Bran was not difficult to find. It is said he was very big. So big that no house nor boat of the day could hold him. He gathered his host, the largest army yet assembled in Britain, to rescue his sister.

The sea between Ireland and Britain was then still young and shallow. Bran waded across carrying the string musicians upon his broad back. So vast was this host, the ship's masts looked like a forest and Bran did seem as a mountain which moved to the Irish watching from the coast. It was Branwen who told them what really came.

Completely outnumbered, the Irish decided to try and console Bran by freeing Branwen and building him the largest house ever. All his adult life, Bran had lived in tents, for no house yet could hold him. It was here that Matholwch should abdicate and crown Gwern as High King of Ireland. But, the Irish had laid a trap.

Warriors hid in hanging flour sacks throughout the large hall. Crafty Evnissyen discovered this and slew them in the bags before the assembly could take place.

Inside, the peace was made and Gwern invested as King. His uncles were anxious to see him and all embraced their young nephew. But, when Evnissyen coaxed him into his grasp, he threw the boy into the roaring fireplace where he burned to death.

Fighting began on all sides and many died as the Host of Bran fought its way out of the huge house. The Irish lit a fire beneath the sacred cauldron and bodies of slain warriors were put into it. They would emerge even more fierce than before, but they were unable to speak.

Seeing the carnage he had started, Evnissyen finally realized what he had done. Wounded, he feigned death among bodies of the slain. Two bare-bottomed Irishmen dropped him in the boiling cauldron. He pushed with all his limbs til the cauldron burst in a tremendous explosion.

One source claims that trees were felled for twenty leagues by the blast. All of the Irish perished save for five pregnant women inside a cave in the wilderness who eventually repopulated Ireland. Of the British, only seven men and Branwen survived.

Bran was dying from a poisoned spear wound. He ordered his own head be severed and carried home on a platter. The head continued to speak and sing, comforting their grief and foretelling the future. When they landed at Anglesey, Branwen died of a broken heart.

On Bran's directions, the men spent seven years in the now empty and derelict Harlech Castle with the Birds of Rhiannon and the head of Bran for company. Eighty years more were thus spent at Gwales in Penvro called the Assembly of the Wondrous Head.

One day, as foretold by Bran, one of the men opened the third door which broke the spell they were under. They then remembered all of their grief. The seven and eighty years became as days and they buried Bran's head per his instructions on White Hill, now called Tower Hill in London.

The head was buried facing the English Channel and while it remained concealed, the island endured no threats nor invasions by sea.

Island Of The Mighty

words and music by Hugin The Bard

Island Of The Mighty

1. The High King of all the Irish
    Sailed from the west so clear
   To the Island of the Mighty
    For Branwen, the daughter of Llyr
   With hair like the wings of blackbirds
    And breasts like the whitest of doves
   The fairest of all of the Ladies
    The mother of Kings to be

2. Together they sailed to Ireland
    After some wounded pride
   Bearing a sacred cauldron
    A face price and Mathaluch's bride
   And Gwern was the son that she bore him
    Of both islands he could be King
   Then one night the words of a drunken man
    A woe to Branwen did bring

3. They forced her to work in the cooking pit
    She toiled for three long years
   And every day the butcher man
    Would box her on one of her ears
   But, one night she rescued a starling
    She nursed it and taught it to speak
   It carried her message to brother Bran
    Who assembled the Host of the King

4. That host was the largest ever
    The islands had ever seen
  They left their homes and their families
    To never again be seen
  In flat-bottom boats crossed the sinking lands
    Where waded the giant Bran
  A forest of trees that the Druids saw
    The coming of the war

5. To put off assured destruction
    They set Branwen free from toil
  And built Bran a house to hold him
    But feelings continued to boil
  To seal the peace with Ireland
    Held feast in the new house of Bran
  Where Evnissyen burned up the child
    And started the war again

C. From the Island of the Mighty
    Unto fair Ireland's shore
  The Host of Bran came boldly
    To fight in the Irish War

6. Matholuch misused the cauldron
    Fed into it parts of the dead
  And from it came demon warriors
    That all of the mortals did dread
  The battle took most of the Irish
    And most of the Host of Bran
  Til Evnissyen finally found honor
    Alive to the cauldron he came

⑦ He hid in a pile of bodies
    Went into the cauldron alive
The cauldron burst with a mighty roar
    And death spread all over the land
And both of the Kings were felled that day
    Of Branwen and those that remained
Only but seven survived that scene
    Among them the head of Bran
They carried the head of Bran
    They talked with the head of Bran

⑧ The seven landed at Anglesey
    Lost Branwen to her broken heart
Then feasted in empty Harlech Castle
    The kingdom now torn apart
Their days were years and for eighty more
    They feasted at Gwales with Bran
They buried his head up on Tower Hill
    And returned to Dyved again

© From the Island of the Mighty
    Unto fair Ireland's shore
The Host of Bran came boldly
    To fight in the Irish War

In that terrible Irish War
In that terrible Irish War

Island Of The Mighty
6/8 TIME

Ⓥ Verse

Dm	C	F	G A	
Dm	C	Dm C	Dm	Dm OPTIONAL :
G	Dm	G	Dm	Dm OPTIONAL :
F	C	Dm C	Dm	Dm OPTIONAL :

Ⓒ Chorus

Dm	C	F	G A
Dm	C	Dm C	Dm
Dm C	Dm	‖ LAST TIME → ‖ Dm C	
Dm C	F G	Dm C	Dm

To add drama and dynamics to this song I usually change tempo to a rapid 4/4 or Common Time during the first chorus and verses six and seven. I then return to 6/8 time for the last verse and chorus

Caswallon's Quarry

(<u>Note</u>: The following tale comes from a variety of sources. It is placed here in context of chronology.)

When the Host of Bran left for Ireland, Caradoc, son of Bran, was left in charge of a council of seven others trusted to govern. While the Host was off to war, a tragic and heinous event took place.

One night at council, a sword appeared to hang in the air. It struck down six of the seven in a matter of moments. Shock, terror and stress from the sudden loss and an inability to combat the flying sword caused a lethal heart attack to the leader of the council. Only Pendaryn Dyved escaped into the night.

Within a cloak of invisibility, Caswallon, son of Beli the former King, had perpetrated a political mass murder in the name of Father-right which resonates to this day.

Among the seven who returned from the war was Pryderi, son of Pwyll and Rhiannon. Once resettled, the young Lord of Dyved came to pay homage to King Caswallon. Late in the honor feast, when Pryderi had had sufficient wine to drink, Caswallon bartered.

While Pryderi lived, the land of Dyved would be taxed no yearly tribute. In exchange, Caswallon could move the sacred circle of standing blue-stones which had been erected by the ancients from Dyved in south Wales to central Britain where they stand today.

Showing the imprudent wisdom of his father, Pryderi basically said, 'If you can move them, you can have them.'

With physics, tools and brute force were they so moved by a large crew of conscripted men. The accompanying song is from one of the nameless who toiled.

Caswallon's Quarry
words and music by Hugin The Bard

c. Farewell my love, my bonny love. I'm bound for the Prescelli Mountains. I hope to come home that you won't be alone. Home from the Prescelli Mountains.

r. I got pulled in the Spring this year, To work in Caswallon's Quar—ry. Here I pull to fulfill my fate, Either to death or to glo—ry.

Caswallon's Quarry

(C) Farewell my love, my bonny love
    I'm bound for the Prescelli Mountains
    I hope to come home that you won't be alone
    Home from the Prescelli Mountains

1. I got pulled in the Spring this year
    To work in Caswallon's Quarry
    Here I pull to fulfill my fate
    Either to death or to glory

    (Chorus)

2. Stones we pull out of old Dyved
    Who tricked Pryderi was Caswallon
    Stones we pull to our own fair land
    That Earth's true magick will carry on

    (Chorus)

3. The hardest pull is the trilithons
    They're tall as a man times three
    Still I pull to return, my love
    Back to my loving family

    (Chorus)

Caswallon's Quarry
4/4 TIME

Ⓒ Chorus

| Dm | G Dm | Dm A | Dm |
| Dm | G Dm | Dm A | Dm |

Ⓥ Verse

| G | Dm | G | A |
| G | Dm | G | A |

Came A Storm

Manawyddan settled in Dyved after the war, married Rhiannon and together they ruled Dyved. Pryderi held title to the land since Pwyll had died. Both he and his young wife Kigva were glad for the love and guidance of the older couple.

One evening after feast, they all went up on the Gorsedd Arberth to sit. Quite suddenly, a thunderstorm descended upon them with fury and a heavy mist. When the storm and mist lifted, all the people, their crops and domestic animals had vanished from Dyved except for the two royal couples.

For two years they lived off stored provisions and wild game. Weary of isolation, they ventured out of Dyved. Manawyddan taught Pryderi to stitch leather and himself learned the arts of gold gilding and blue enamelling called Calch Llasar. Good it was that they learned trades, for when Pryderi looked into the bag of gold he'd carried from Dyved, he found only dried up oak leaves.

In one town they made saddles. In another, shields. In a third town they made boots. In each place the same thing happened. So pleasing were their goods with gold and blue trim that other merchants of the same trade could sell none of their own goods. The merchants conspired to kill them in their sleep. Three times forewarned and three times escaped, they returned to Dyved.

Though warriors such as Manawyddan and Pryderi

could easily have fought off merchants, they chose to flee. Political intrigue following the war was still active and none could tell how Caswallon might respond to a situation like this.

One day while hunting, the men encountered a white boar. The hounds chased it into a marvelous fortress where no fortress had stood before. Pryderi pursued them. Inside, he found a golden bowl hung by gold chains over a marble slab. When he touched it, he could no longer move nor speak. When Rhiannon heard of this, she went after her son and met the same fate. At that, the fortress vanished from sight.

Manawyddan and Kigva went back to Britain and made shoes til they met the same treatment as before. A year and a day from their departure, they once again returned to Dyved. They brought back a load of wheat and sowed three fields of it. When the wheat was ready to harvest, they found the stalks broken off with none of the tops to be found in the first field. Next day they found the second field in the same condition. That night they guarded the third field.

At midnight a tumult arose. A host of mice was stealing the harvest. They were very fast mice. But, Manawyddan spied a large and slightly slower mouse than the rest and caught it. Imprisoned in his glove, he took it next morning to Gorsedd Arberth where he erected a tiny scaffold on which to hang and execute the captured thief.

After seven years of seeing no others in Dyved,

Manawyddan was curious to see a threadbare Bard approach as he worked. The Bard offered silver to spare the mouse. Manawyddan refused. Next, a Druid came by offering gold. Again, he refused. Finally, a High Druid with retinue came to the sight of execution. The noose was now around the prisoner's neck. After refusing an enormous amount of wealth and goods, Manawyddan was asked to name his terms. He bargained well.

He asked for and received the release of Rhiannon and Pryderi, removal of the enchantment spell from all of Dyved, that no revenge ever be taken for the results of the current negotiations nor for any past acts committed by anyone of Dyved and last of all he wanted an explanation.

The High Druid was actually Llwd, the Gray Man of Rhiannon's former realm. The enchantment spell over Dyved was for the violence done to Gwawl during the game of Badger In The Bag at Pwyll's wedding to Rhiannon. The inhabitants of Dyved, now returned, had been turned into flying insects. The wheat was taken by Llwd's court members while magickally transformed into mice. The captured mouse was the pregnant wife of Llwd. This was why Manawyddan could acquire all of his terms.

During confinement, Pryderi had to bear about his neck the great gate hammers of Llwd's fortress and Rhiannon bore the collars of asses after they had carried hay. For this reason, some refer to this story as The Mabinogi Of The Hay Collars And Gate Hammers.

Came A Storm

From the Gorsedd Arberth unto Dyved came a storm

1. It followed Queen Rhiannon from her bright world
   To the land where she had come
   Once King Pwyll was dead and gone
   And the land was no longer protected by Arawn

2. It turned all the people into butterflies
   And their fields were all laid bare
   Only wild things anywhere
   Just the four of Dyved's royal family left to care

3. The four were lonely so, they ventured forth
   And the men did learn a trade
   Gilded saddles and boots they made
   For Dyved's gold turned to old dried up leaves inside the bag

4. Their goods were special, being gilt in gold
   With blue calch llasar in their way
   That other merchants had no pay
   Forced the family to flee back to Dyved or else be slain

5. One day in the Spring out with the hunting dogs
   They encountered a snow white boar
   It led the pack into the Gorsedd door
   Once it lured both Pryderi and Rhiannon, closed with a roar

6. Manawyddan and Kigva spent a year away
   Planted wheat fields near the house
   Then they captured a thieving mouse
   For the loss of their crops they would hang that thieving mouse

⑦ The Gray One pleaded for that pregnant mouse
For the mouse was in fact his wife
So he bargained to end her strife
In exchange he returned all of Dyved back to life

From the Gorsedd Arberth unto Dyved came a storm

Came A Storm
4/4 TIME

Refrain:

| Em | D | G | A |
| Em7 | Em7 | Em7 | Em7 |

Ⓥ Verse

Em	D	Em D	Em
A	A	Em7	Em7
A	A	Em7	Em7
D	G	B7	B7
Em7	Em7	Em7	Em7

The Pigs of Pryderi

Math ap Mathonwy was Lord of Gwynedd in the north of Wales when Pryderi ruled Dyved in the south. His nephew longed for Goewin, the King's footmaiden. So, one of his other nephews, Gwydion, devised a plan to aid the lovestruck Gilvaethwy.

He got the King's permission to journey into Dyved in order to acquire some of the tasty new livestock there called both pigs and swine. These domestic pigs were gifts to the folk of Dyved from Arawn, Lord of Annwn, in the underworld.

Gwydion, Gilvaethwy and ten of their friends dressed as musicians and went to Pryderi's court. Now, Gwydion was the best teller of tales in the world and he entertained well that night. Before retiring, he asked Pryderi for the pigs. But, he could neither sell nor give them away til they had doubled their number, per Arawn's instructions.

That night Gwydion gathered fungi and toadstools of the forest. By magick arts did he transform them into twelve magnificent horses and twelve handsome greyhounds with bridles, collars and gear, the metal parts being of solid gold. In the morning they were presented as exchange for the sweet tasting pigs.

After holding council, those of Dyved agreed to the exchange. Gwydion and his men took the pigs and went swiftly home. The enchantment upon the goods left in exchange would last only one day, then they would be as they originally were. The places they stopped on that journey are to this day called Mochdrev and Mochnant which mean pig town and pig brook. The pigs were left in a safe place.

When the men returned to court, the Host of Gwynedd was preparing to do battle with the Host of Dyved come for Gwydion and the stolen pigs. After council as to where to force the fight, Gwydion and Gilvaethwy returned to Caer Dathyl. With the King at the field of battle, Gwydion chased the women from Math's chamber and there his brother had his way with Goewin against her will.

In the morning, battle was joined and many on both sides perished. Truce was called and the men of Dyved began marching home escorted by the Host of Gwynedd. When they reached the ford called Velenryd, the footsoldiers began fighting again.

Pryderi called for and received single combat with Gwydion, whom he felt was responsible for the war. The armies stood back while the fierce duel took place. With both strength and magick, Gwydion prevailed and there Pryderi was buried. The nephews of Math rode the circuit of Gwynedd as was custom after victorious battle.

When Math founs his footholder no longer a maiden, he married her giving her to rule Gwynedd. He then decreed that none shall give food nor water to the two rapists. They finally returned to court to face their punishment.

For three years they were to live as wild beasts. By

magick wand, Math turned Gilvaethwy into a hind and Gwydion into a stag. The second year, the hind became a boar and the stag became a wild sow. Third year, the sow was transformed into a he~wolf and the boar into a she~wolf.

At the end of each year, the animals returned with an offspring which Math turned into human youths with his magick wand. At the end of the third year, their punishment served, Math turned them back into Gwydion and Gilvaethwy and welcomed them back into his court.

The Pigs Of Pryderi

words and music by Hugin The Bard

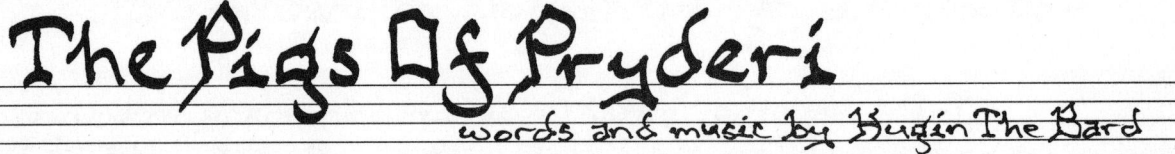

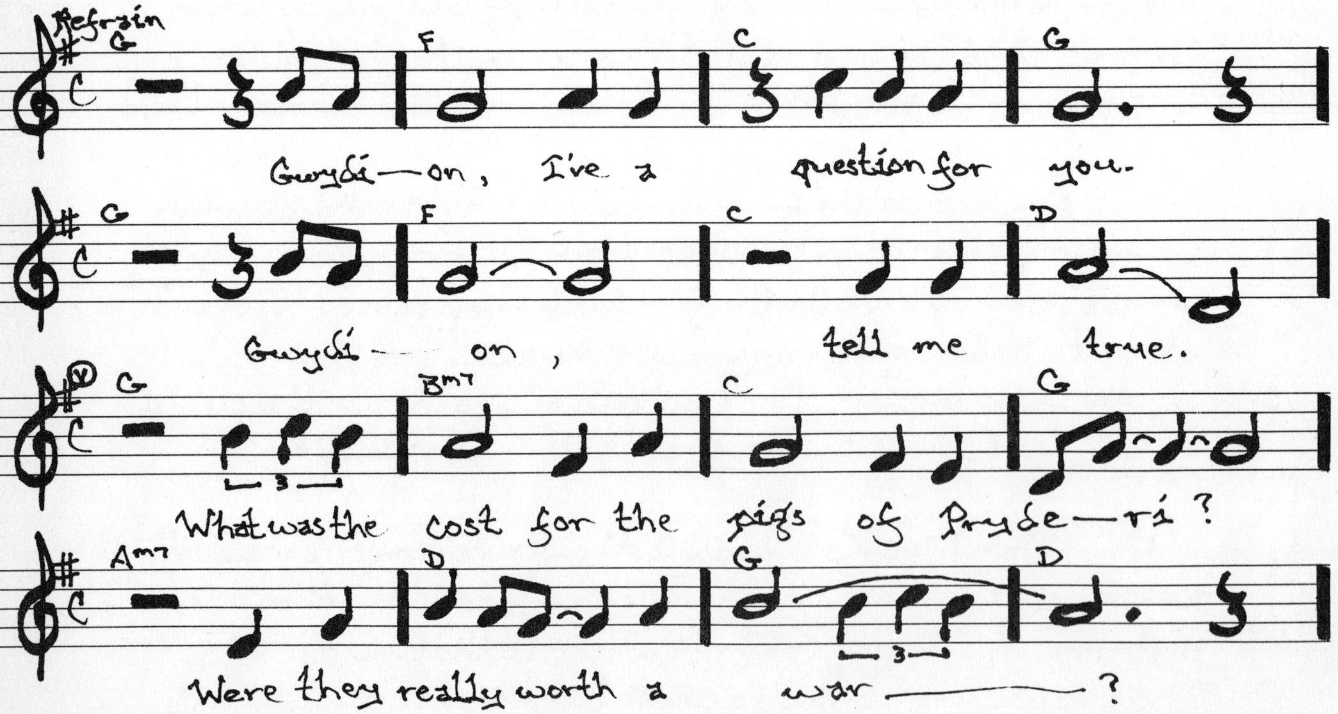
Refrain
G F C G
Gwydi — on, I've a question for you.
G F C D
Gwydi — on, tell me true.
G Bm7 C G
What was the cost for the pigs of Pryde — ri?
Am7 D G D
Were they really worth a war ——?

The Pigs of Pryderi

(Refrain)
Gwydion, I've a question for you. Gwydion, tell me true,

1. What was the cost for the pigs of Pryderi?
   Were they really worth a war?
   What was the fee for your brother's longing?
   Was it worth three years or more?
   For you did deceive your uncle
   Brought dishonor to his door
   You helped to rape the King's footmaiden
   While the King was out to war
   What did you gain from your wily magick?
   Did you learn what you went for?

2. You were sublime with your tales and singing
   As a minstrel in Dyved
   Trading twelve horses and a dozen greyhounds
   All with golden tack for just twelve pigs
   Then you left in quite a hurry
   To get far out of Dyved
   Next day when your magick faded
   Fungus were their goods instead
   You made a war with an honest people
   Now there would be many dead

3. You won the duel at the Velenryd
   Half of all the armies slain
   You won the war, but you lost your body
   Math the Ancient plays no game
   Live a year as a stag
   Live a year as a sow
   Live a year as a wild wolf
   Up the evolution chain

49

What did you think of your beast-bred children?
Will you ever be the same?
(Refrain)
Gwydion, I've a question for you. Gwydion, tell me true
What was the cost for the pigs of Pryderi?
Were they really worth a war?

The Pigs Of Pryderi
4/4 TIME

(Refrain)

| G | F | C | G | G | F | C | D |

Ⓥ Verse

G	Bm7	C	G	Am7	D	G	D
G	Bm7	C	G	Am7	D	G C	G
F	C	G	G	F	C	D	D
F	C	G	G	F	C	D	D
G	Bm7	C	G	Am7	D	G C	G D

(Refrain)

| G | F | C | G | G | F | C | D |
| G | Bm7 | C | G | Am7 | D | G C | G |

(Part II)
Children of Dôn

Dôn is another name for Danu or Dana, the Great Mother. She is spoken of when we refer to the Tuatha De Danaan who are also called the People of Danu. These light skinned and fair haired matriarchal people came to the British Isles about 1500 b.c.e. from across the sea. Where they came from is not agreed upon by scholars.

Some think they were Greeks or Phoenicians from an island named Danu in the Aegean Sea which was vacated about the same time. Others say they came from the valley of the Danube River, named for the Goddess Danu, in what is now Germany. Still others believe they were remnants from the island civilization of fabled Atlantis.

Settling in parts of Wales and Ireland, they moved out the local Picts and Fomorians, sometimes by force. They were firmly established when the first wave of Celtic peoples arrived. Though the Irish later masculanized Dôn, the Welsh kept her as their Mother Goddess.

We here go in depth with only a few of her brood. Bountiful is the harvest for those who pursue and learn the myths and tales of those folk from the sea.

Children Of Dôn

1. Many years ago in the land of Gwynedd
   Was a family that ruled for so long
   In the memory of man then like Gods they became
   And we call them the Children of Dôn

2. Fair Dôn was the mother of many healthy babes
   And she was sister to the King
   Mother-right was the law of the land
   To her would be born the next King

3. That King would be Gwydion, a trickster and magician
   A warrior, a scholar and Bard
   And the sister he loved most in her castle by the sea
   Was the beautiful Arianrhod

C. Children of Dôn go on and on
   Those of the folk from the sea
   Children of Dôn go on and on
   And live in our memory

4. Then there was Govannon, the smith at his forge
   And Lord of Fields, Amaethon
   With Gilvaethwy were brothers to three sisters more
   Demure Eillen, Penardim and faire Maelan

5. When a brother tricked a sister into bearing family
   One of whom would be a future King
   They had battles and children and farther they strayed
   From the Ancient Harmonies

[C] Children of Don go on and on
Those of the folk from the sea
Children of Don go on and on
And live in our memory

Children of Dôn
4/4 TIME

[V] Verse

D	D	Em7	Em7
G	G	D	D
D	D	Em7	Em7
A	A	D	D

[C] Chorus

G	A	D	Bm
G	D	A	A
G	A	D	Bm
Em7	D	C	C
A	A

On The Wind

Brother to Danu was Math the Ancient who outlived all other first generation Tuatha De Danaan. Highly skilled in the Art Magickal, he ruled Gwynedd from his stronghold at Caer Dathyl. In old age, he spent most of his time seated in meditation with his feet in the lap of a virgin maiden, only leaving in times of war.

He was known for his wisdom and fairness, even to the point of disciplining his own royal relatives when warranted. When those deep gray eyes looked out from his ancient face framed by long white hair and beard, you just knew that he could see right through everything about you. Looking into them seemed to behold the very depths of the sea and the eternity of the past.

The psychic ability of Math was developed to a degree perhaps never since reached by any mortal. Honesty prevailed in Gwynedd, for Math could sense the words and dreams and even the thoughts of anyone he chose within his realm. Very few of the common people really understood this. To them, their words were carried to his ears on the wind.

On The Wind

words and music by Hugin The Bard

On The Wind

① Wise old King with beard so long
   How long ago were you born?
   So still like a mountain upon the throne
   Hearing our thoughts on the wind

② Fair to your subjects and wise to your kin
   Master of magick and time
   Reading the minds of the folk as they dream
   Carried to you on the wind

[C] Brother to Danu who came from the sea
    Son of Mathonwy

③ Leader of battles and loser of none
   You were the Lord of the land
   You knew the tale that sexes were once one
   Drifting apart on the wind

④ Time was a concept to you not so old
   You knew it all in the end
   Women and men will grow closer again
   Talking to you on the wind

[C] Brother to Danu who came from the sea
    Son of Mathonwy

⑤ Wise old King with beard so long
   How long ago were you born?
   So still like a mountain upon the throne
   Hearing our thoughts on the wind

On The Wind
4/4 TIME

Ⓥ Verse

Em7	Em7	D	Em7
D	D	Em7	Em7
Em7	Em7	D	Em7
D	D	Em7	Em7
D	D	Em7	Em7

Ⓒ Chorus

| G | D | C | Em7 |
| C | B7 | Em9 | Em9 |

Note: Last line of each verse repeats once. Also, the last vocal note of the Chorus is the ninth of the chord. So, you have the option of playing either Em9 or Em7.

The Dreams of Arianhrod

Following the war over the Pigs of Pryderi, Math married his footholder, Goewin, making her Queen over Gwynedd. For some reason, it was important to Math's meditations that his footholder be a virgin maiden and that position was now vacant.

Gwydion travelled to the coastal castle, called The Silver Wheel, where lived his favorite sister, Arianhrod. He persuaded her to try to become the King's new footholder. There she would be at the center of social, fashion and political life in Gwynedd. Gwydion knew that his adolescent sister had become enamored with a self-identity of being a virgin as understood by the new tribe, the Celts of southern Wales.

To the Tuatha De Danaan, a virgin was merely an unmarried woman. But, when the new tribe said virgin, they meant a true maiden. Gwydion also knew personally that his sister was not that kind of virgin.

Arianhrod and her castle now host an eternal feast in the sky for the souls of priesthood, royalty and the very best musicians and Bards who have passed from this life to the other side of the veil between life and death.

The Dreams Of Arianhrod

words and music by Hugin The Bard

The Dreams Of Arianrhod

1. There once was a fair young lady
   Who wanted to try things new
   She thought she would be a virgin
   As if it were something to do

2. The word had a brand new meaning
   Brought in from the new tribe
   Instead of an unmarried lady
   'Twas a maiden truly inside

1.C Such were the dreams of Arianrhod
   In her castle by the sea
   But, a woman's no longer a virgin
   Who knows what a man can be

3. This lady once loved a brother
   And a Lord from under the sea
   Though she used women's wisdom
   To prevent any pregnancy

4. She sought a role as a virgin
   To be footholder of the King
   But, when she stepped over the Magic Wand
   Two children came into being

1.C Such were the dreams of Arianrhod
   In her castle by the sea
   But, a woman's no longer a virgin
   Who knows what a man can be

5. Son Dylan, he swam away then
   Llew was raised by Gwydion
   Dylan died at Govannon's hand
   But, the tale of Llew went on

6. She finally died with her castle
   Was reborn in Arawn's realm
   Now, she hosts a forever feast
   A hostess to overwhelm

2.C Such are the dreams of Arianrhod
   In her castle in the sky
   Feasting with Bards and Priests and Kings
   Who go there when they die

7. She sits at the head of the table
   In her castle in the sky
   Don't be surprised if Arawn
   Is right there by her side

8. Starlight shines like a rainbow
   Through the crystalline walls
   Music played by the finest Bards
   Taliesen the best of all

2.E Such are the dreams of Arianrhod
   In her castle in the sky
   Feasting with Bards and Priests and Kings
   Who go there when they die

The Dreams Of Arianhrod
4/4 TIME

Ⓥ Verse

Dm	C	Dm	Dm
G	F	Dm	Dm
Dm	C	F	G
Dm	C	Dm	Dm

Ⓒ Chorus

G	Dm	A	Dm
G	Dm	A	A
Dm	C	F	G
Dm	C	Dm	Dm

A Very Funny Man

Arianhrod's most famous son was Llew Llaw Gyffes. His tale is anything but ordinary.

A Very Funny Man

[C] Oh, Llew Llaw Gyffes was a very funny man
Yes, a very funny man, indeed!

(1.) He was born as a zygote
Incubated in a trunk
Had a fight with his mother right away
He got married to a girl
Made out of flowers
He was murdered
Changed his shape and almost died

(2.) He was bright as the Sun
He knew magick and dreams
And late in his life was the King
Was a master at chess
Anything he would do
Had the magick
Of Gwydion's Line

[C] Oh, Llew Llaw Gyffes was a very funny man
Yes, a very funny man, indeed!

(3.) It took the longest of time
For them to give him a name
Or the weapons of being an adult
And his mother never let him
Go out with normal girls
He had to find his girlfriends
In the flower bed

④ The lover of his wife
   Is the guy that murdered him
   But, he didn't die, he turned into a bird
   An eagle with a wound
   Sort of an ill eagle ate by pigs
   Til his father healed him
   With a song

C Ah, Llew Llaw Gyffes was a very funny man
   Yes, a very funny man, indeed!

⑤ He lived a very
   Strange life, indeed!
   And after life they made him a God
   A God of the Sun
   And after hearing this song
   I hope he has
   A great sense of humor

C Ah, Llew Llaw Gyffes was a very funny man
   Yes, a very funny man, indeed!

A Very Funny Man
4/4 TIME

[C] Chorus

| C | G | C | D |
| D | D | D | |

[V] Verse

G	G	A	A
F	F	G	G
G	G	A	A
F	F	G	G

Note: I do this song very much up-tempo. The words are spoken rather than sung and I alter my voice to sound silly and funny.

Lady, My Lady

At Arianrhod's virginity trial, she didn't know that she bore two. Glad she was that Dylan swam off. But, Gwydion hastened the other raw young thing to his chamber where he grew the lad in a special trunk at the foot of his bed with magick and chants and herbs, til the proper time for his birth.

And there came the time when the lad needed a name by his mother, as was the custom. So, Gwydion and the boy went to Arianrhod's castle by the sea. But, she was not pleased. Her embarrassment still stung her pride deeply and she vowed he would not be named until that name was given by her. And the look in her eye showed she had no intention of doing so. But, Gwydion had at least a few tricks up his sleeve and one day they came to the castle in disguise....

① Lady, my Lady, we are bootmakers
The best in the land
Won't you come down that I may fit your feet
Place them in my hands
When she came down to their boat
At a bird the lad took aim and threw a stone
She gasped, "Did you see little sure shot?"
Llew Llaw Gyffes (The Lion with the steady hand)

"Thank you, my Lady. Your son now has a name." Then the boot leather turned to seaweed and the boat to driftwood and the bootmaker and his son became Gwydion and young Llew all released from Gwydion's magick charm.

Arianhrod was not pleased.

"My brother, you've tricked me again. How could you be so cruel?"

"'Twas your cruelty to the boy that brought me to this deed."

"Ahh!", she cried. Then she turned and grinned and said, "Well, I know this much. He'll never receive the arms of manhood and therefore, never sit on the throne as King unless those weapons are placed upon him by his mother. This I vow!" And the look in her eye showed she had no intention of doing so. So, another day they came to her castle in disguise, this time as musicians.....

② Lady, my Lady, we are wandering Bards
   May we play for you
   We know songs of wonder, we know tales and more
   At your feast for you
   In the morning came an invasion
   To help you, we must have arms
   Lady, I know my business
   Help arm the boy (And so she did.)

"Thank you, my Lady. The invasion has gone and your son now has arms." At this the musicians became Gwydion and young Llew. Arianhrod was not pleased!

"Ah, my brother, how could you do this to me? A shame upon you and a shame upon me for being tricked again by the brother I once loved above all things. Ahh! You've left me but one move. I swear by the Mother that this lad shall never know the love and embrace of mortal woman born of this Earth. This is my final vow to you!" And she never again left her castle.

Well, this problem stumped even Gwydion. Arianrhod's magick was as powerful as his own. So, he went to his uncle, the King, Math the Ancient, whose magick was the most powerful in the land. And together the King and Gwydion, who was both father and uncle to Llew, created for him a bride not born of woman, but made of magick and flowers. Ah, but that's another tale entirely.

③ Lady, my Lady of the Silver Wheel
   Passing on into night
   You will be together with your brother love
   And your son so bright
   When they pass from this plane of restriction
   To your castle in the sky

Lady, My Lady

words and music by Hugin The Bard

(Note: The rest of the verse is spoken without music.)
(Verse is written an octave higher than actually sung.)
and threw a stone. She gasped! Did you see Little
Sure Shot? Llew Llaw Gyffes (The Lion with the steady hand)

Blodeuwedd

They named her Blodeuwedd and she was lovely. Her flesh had been fashioned from the blooms of oak, broom and meadowsweet. The magickal means of providing her even the most simple or unevolved spirit can only be guessed at today. Wed to Llew the day after her creation, they moved to the lovely cantrevs around Ardudwy.

One day Llew left to visit Math. That evening, a hunter and his men sought refuge at Ardudwy Castle and Blodeuwedd and the hunter, Goronwy Pevr, fell in love. So blind and strong was their love that they conspired for Blodeuwedd to discover from Llew the only way to defeat the protective magick of his family and for Goronwy to kill him and rule in his place. Having done so, Goronwy used magick to appear as Llew, thinking that no one knew.

But, Gwydion knew something was up. He eventually found Llew and restored him to health. Llew then killed Goronwy in the same place he had been attacked by Goronwy, casting a spear through a stone that Goronwy held as a shield. Gwydion pursued Blodeuwedd into the mountains where he caught her and turned her into an owl.

To this day in parts of Ireland and Wales an owl is still called a Blodeuwedd.

Blodeuwedd

words and music by Hugin The Bard

Blodeuwedd

1. Fashioned from flowers, a magickal birth
   A gift for the Prince from the King
   Fairer than flowers that grow on the Earth
   Beautiful Lady, I sing

2. Blossoms of oak, broom and meadowsweet
   Were brought to the King and Gwydion
   Where in the King's chamber three days did retreat
   And brought you forth when they were done

3. Wed the next day to Llew Llaw, hand in hand
   Heir to the King of Gwynedd
   The fairest of Cantrevs would be your land
   In Ardudwy, fair Blodeuwedd

4. Happy you seemed til your Lord went away
   To visit the King and his kin
   Through magick and cunning then did you betray
   Young Llew, for a man you let in

C. Blodeuwedd, who are you?
   Blodeuwedd, you are Whoo!

5. How could a maiden so fair and so bright
   Do what you did to your man?
   With Goronwy Pevr, your lover by night
   Slew young Llew Llaw, the sure hand

6. By magick, that bandit and Llew looked the same
   Though Goronwy added a scowl
   But, you met your maker when Gwydion came
   And turned you then into an owl

V. As you take wing on a fanciful flight
   Over the fields of Gwynedd
   Feeding on creatures that stir in the night
   Do you know now, Blodeuwedd?

C. Blodeuwedd, who are you?
   Blodeuwedd, you are Whoo!

Blodeuwedd
3/4 TIME

V. Verse

D	D/C#	Bm	F#m
G	Bm	A	A
D	D/C#	Bm	F#m
Em7	A	D	D

C. Chorus

| Em7 | G | F#m | Bm |
| G | Bm | A | A |

The Cauldron And The Goat

The manner in which Llew was murdered and resurrected seemed so strange that I felt compelled to write a silly song about it.

Llew could only be killed by a magick spear constructed only on the Full Moons over the course of a year. For the spear to be effective, Llew must be standing with one foot on a billy goat and the other foot on the edge of a bath size cauldron under a thatched roof with no walls by the bank of a river such as originally served as moats for early castles.

The conspirators managed to pull all this off and the body of Llew transformed into an eagle which flew off.

A couple of months later, Gwydion discovered the bird high in an oak tree. The bird's flesh, putrified from the spear wound, would drop to the ground where a pig made feast of it. Gwydion changed the eagle back into Llew by singing it a song.

The Cauldron And The Goat
(To the tune of "Farmer In The Dell")

1. The cauldron and the goat
   The castle and the moat
   Fooled by Blodeuwedd
   Wearin' no coat

2. You know she had your ear
   The spear took a year
   Made on the Full Moons
   Don't you feel queer?

3. He waited for your bath
   And hid up the path
   The only time the magick failed
   Do you feel wrath?

4. He got you in sight
   And slew you so bright
   And you were no more a man
   An eagle took flight

5. Til Daddy came along
   And sang you a song
   And now that story told
   End of this song

An Oak Grows

When Llew disappeared, Gwydion could tell that Goronwy Peur had taken the appearance and place of Llew. Despite their combined magick, niether Gwydion nor Math could find Llew anywhere. For Llew was no longer a man, but had become an eagle and flown off when pierced by the magick spear cast by Goronwy. His mind had become that of the eagle. But, Gwydion did not yet know this.

To search for Llew, Gwydion travelled in the guise of a minstrel or Bard as he had done before when he wished to travel the land freely and without being recognized. This provided a number of advantages. For it was an unwritten law of the Ancient Harmonies that travelling musicians be given food and shelter wherever they go. In exchange, the host would receive entertainment and news of events and fashions from the places the musicians had travelled.

Gwydion searched the lands of Gwynedd and Powys through the Autumn to Midwinter. His search was slow for he left no stone unturned. No bush was too small to be searched by his Druid sight. He paid special attention to birds and other flying creatures. For the Druids of that day taught that the souls of the departed often took the form of flying things to aid their travels on the wind.

That night he stayed at a farm near Maenor Penardd, the place of the battle between the men of Gwynedd and Dyved for the Pigs of Pryderi which Gwydion had stolen so long ago. This farm had on it a sow that would not eat with the other animals. Rather, it would run away each morning to return at sunset. Yet, she and her piglets seemed well fed. In the morning, Gwydion followed the sow to the base of an old oak tree where she began to eat.

It was by the River Cynvael, the same stream where Pryderi had died by Gwydion's hand. Pryderi's last words were that Gwydion's flesh should be eaten by the swine he had stolen.

The vengeance of that dying curse was hard upon Gwydion. For high in the oak perched an eagle looking not at all well. Pieces of its decaying flesh dropped to the ground and became the pig's meal. When Gwydion had overcome his grief, he began to sing to the bird on high that he knew was Llew.

1. Between two lakes an oak grows
   Dark it stands o'er sky and glen
   If I speak not untruth
   Here do I gaze upon Llew

The bird was drawn to the sweet voice and it came down to a lower branch.

2. Within high ground an oak grows
   Rain and heat doth age it on
   If I speak not untruth
   There in the branches is Llew Llaw Gyffes

That name stirred forgotten memories within the bird and it came down the lowest branch of the tree.

3. Upon a slope an oak grows
   Tall and regal grows the tree

If I speak not untruth
Llew will come to my knee

    The bird flew down to Gwydion and when touched by his magick wand, became the wounded body of Llew. The healing took long for the wounds were grievous and it was the next Midwinter before Llew dealt with Goronwy and Gwydion dealt with Blodeuwedd.

An Oak Grows

Cad Goddeu

A tale comes to us from "The Romance of Taliesen" (Taliesen was a sixth century Bard) of a fantastic battle in which Gwydion defeated Bran by making the trees of the forest come to animated life and fight the battle as his army. It is said that seventy-one thousand perished in that battle.

Arrayed with Bran was Arawn and the forces of Annwn, the underworld. Among that host was said to be such creatures as a hundred-headed beast, a black toad with a hundred claws and a snake of many colors within whose flesh were a hundred tormented souls. Bran, known for his great size, was said to carry a brigade of fighters under his tongue root and another brigade behind his head.

With Gwydion were the other sons of Dôn, his son Llew and the Lady Achren (Trees).

Gwydion's forces could not be defeated lest the name of Lady Achren be guessed. So too, could Arawn's host only be defeated by guessing the name of Bran which Gwydion did through the magick of the trees.

It is said by many scholars that this was no ordinary warfare, but rather a battle of wits and scholarship. This idea is supported by the guessing of the names for victory and by the fact that to the learned Druids and priests of the Tuatha De Danaan was known an alphabet whose letter names were the names of trees. This alphabet was called Ogham after its creator, the sun-god Ogma.

Ogham was rarely used in full script. Each character communicated several ideas and situations as well as naming a tree. Each letter referred to the characteristics and uses of that tree.

The alphabet could be used in many ways. It could be scribed on beech tablets (Beech is the root of our word book). It could be notched on sticks and stones or conveyed through finger code across the shin or nose and by pointing to places on the hand. As such, it was quite functional as a secret code which the Christians tried to suppress. It could also be used as a system of divination and remained in use until at least the sixth century by Celtic monks.

Living much more closely to nature than we do today, trees were especially sacred beings to the Tuatha De Danaan and their spirituality. Their use of the word trees included many bushes, vines and grasses, plants we define differently today.

Gwydion used the trees to defeat Bran. That is, he guessed Bran's name by the Alder branch in Bran's hand (maybe on his shield). But, why was the battle fought?

It was fought to acquire for the Tuatha De Danaan three boons from the underworld. Gwydion's brother, Amaethon, Lord of Fields, went to Annwn to acquire the boons. Some say he stole them from Arawn. Thus the battle for their possession.

The three boons were....

✦ The Dog, a guardian! But, not just any dog. A dog from the underworld, much like the Greek, Cerberus, who guarded the entrance to Hades.

✦ The Lapwing, a disguiser! A bird who nests on open ground and feigns a broken wing to draw away from the nest any intruders or threats to its progeny. The Koran says King Solomon trusted it.

✦ The White Roebuck, a wonder! Many a King in the olde tales did pursue a stag like this into the forest to find a wonder or death. It is said to be symbolic of our journey from this life to the next.

Analysis of this tale can be without end for each answer produces another question. So, experience the tale and let the mysteries happen within

Cad Goddeu (Battle Of The Trees)
Based on the translation by Robert Graves

1. The tops of the Beech tree
    Have sprouted of late
   Are changed and renewed
    From their withered state
   When the Beech prospers
    Though spells and Litanies
   The Oak tops entangle
    There is hope for the trees

2. I have plundered the Fern
    Through all secrets I spy
   Old Math ap Mathonwy
    Knew no more than I
   For with nine sorts of faculty
    God has gifted me
   I am fruit of fruits gathered
    From nine sorts of tree

3. Plum, Quince, Whortle, Mulberry
    Raspberry, Pear
   Black Cherry and White
    With the Sorb in me share
   From my seat at Fefynedd
    A city that is strong
   I watched the trees and green things
    Hastening along

4) Retreating from happiness
    They would fain be set
In forms of the chief letters
    Of the alphabet
Wayfarers wondered
    Warriors were dismayed
At renewal of conflicts
    Such as Gwydion made

5) Under the tongue root
    A fight most dread
And another raging
    Behind, in the head
The Alders in the front line
    Began the affray
Willow and Rowan tree
    Were tardy in array

6) The Holly, dark green
    Made a resolute stand
He is armed with many spear points
    Wounding the hand
With footbeat of the swift Oak
    Heaven and Earth rung
'Stout Guardian of the Door'
    His name in every tongue

7. Great was the Gorse in battle
     And the Ivy at her prime
   The Hazel was arbiter
     At this charmed time
   Uncouth and savage was the Fir
     Cruel the Ash tree
   Turns not aside a footbreadth
     Straight at the heart runs she

8. The Birch, though very noble
     Armed himself, but late
   A sign not of cowardice
     But, of high estate
   The Heath gave consolation
     To the toil spent folk
   The long enduring Poplars
     In battle much broke

9. Some of them were cast away
     On the field of fight
   Because of holes torn in them
     By the enemy's might
   Very wrathful was the Vine
     Whose henchmen are the Elms
   I exalt him mightily
     To rulers of realms

10. Strong chieftains were the Blackthorn
       With his ill fruit
    The unbeloved Whitethorn
       Who bears the same suit
    The swift pursuing Reed
       The Broom with her brood
    And the Furze but ill-behaved
       Until he is subdued

11. The sower scattering Yew
       Stood glum at the fight's fringe
    With the Elder slow to burn
       Amid fires that singe
    And the blessed Wild Apple
       Laughing in pride
    From the Gorcham of Maeldrew
       By the rock side

12. In shelter linger
       Privet and Woodbine
    Inexperienced in warfare
       And the courtly Pine
    But I, although slighted
       Because I was not big
    Fought, trees, in your array
       On the fields of Godden Brig

13. From my seat at Fefynedd
    A city that is strong
I watched the trees and green things
    Hastening along
But I, although slighted
    Because I was not big
Fought, trees, in your array
    In the fields of Godden Brig

Cad Goddeu (Battle Of The Trees)
2/4 TIME

V. Verse

Em	Em	D	Em
Em	Em	D	Em
Em	Em	D	Em
Em	Em	D	A
Em	Em	Em	A G

Note: Last two measures optional instrumental.

Feasting The Wheel

The customs and traditions presented in these songs are by no means the only ones. Though the Wheel is enclosed in a circle, it is always open to interpretation.

Dance, song, food, tales, lore and socializing are all elements of feasting. The Bard knows that feasting is a form of worship just as important and valid as all the solemn invocations and properly performed actions of high priesthood.

Too many times I've seen a ritual conclude with the phrase, "That's it ~ Let's eat!", as if the serious business of worship were over and the real reason for congregating could commence.

Let not your communion with Deity terminate at the close of formal ritual. Rather, carry it with you as the admirable Tibetan Buddhists who strive to make every breath a prayer.

In the words of The Goddess, "All acts of love and pleasure are My rituals."

The Wheel

The eight spoked wheel or Wheel of the Year is a symbol used by many peoples. From the Druids of ancient Europe to present day Buddhists and Neo-Pagans, this symbol generally represents the cyclic progression of time.

Whether one chooses to see a map of the solar year, a layout of ritual tools or a schedule for the wearing of specific stones, the Wheel is easy to embrace. Pleasing and balanced to the eye, it conveys motion.

This musical journey of the Wheel will stop at each of the eight Pagan High Days or Sabbats. They happen at the times of solar extremes and balance, the Solstices and Equinoxes, and the four points mid-way between each Solstice and Equinox.

The Wheel

words and music by Hugin The Bard

The Wheel

C Learn the ways of the wheel
   The wheel is always turning
   Live the love within the wheel
   A lover's always learning

1 Come in perfect love and trust
   Come then without fear
   Ash to ash or dust to dust
   The wheel is always here

2 The sabbats that we celebrate
   Show life within the year
   The symbols that they represent
   Show life beyond what's here

(Chorus)

3 Eight High Days and sacred ways
   To reach the Gods above
   Eight magick tools and shining jewels
   To manifest our love

4 Thirteen moons and a day
   Is what they call a year
   In a year and a day
   The wheel will be back here

(Chorus)

5) Come in perfect love and trust
   Come then without fear
   Ash to ash or dust to dust
   The wheel is always here

(The Wheel)
   6/8 TIME

C Chorus

| E | A E | D | A E |
| E | A E | D | A E |

V Verse

| G | D | C | G |
| E | D | C D | E |

After the verse, I suggest this line as fill.

| E | A E | D | A E |

<u>Watch The Wheel Turn</u>

December 21st is generally known as the date of the Winter Solstice or Yule. The actual moment of Solstice can be as much as 36 hours on either side of this date by our current calendar. In the northern hemisphere, the days are short and the nights are long. The Earth seems to sleep. It is the longest night of the year.

This night holds the promise of brighter and more fertile times. The Sun is, in a sense, reborn. It will grow and mature, culminating in the other Solstice and those long days of Summer.

Knowing that promise helped ancient Pagans survive dark winters. A Midwinter feast also gave benefits to the diet as surely as to the spirit.

Watch the Wheel Turn (Yule)

words and music by Hugin The Bard

Watch The Wheel Turn

1. Beautiful baby child
   Born on a cold winter's night
   Filled with the promise of life
   And the promise of enduring light

2. Magickal Mother mighty
   Bringer of life to the Earth
   Beautiful Lady in white
   Giving the Sun its rebirth

B. Though the night is cold and dark
   The longest of the year
   We meet within the circle now
   In worship and good cheer

C. Amid the holly and the ivy
   Watch the wheel turn
   Meet me in the circle
   Let the Yule log burn
   Everybody's happy
   Trying last year's mead
   If you stand beneath the mistletoe
   You'll get kissed, indeed!

3. Here where the wheel begins
   We start on a journey of the year
   All that can happen in life
   Is found in the wheel of the year

(Bridge)

(Chorus)

(Watch The Wheel Turn)
4/4 Time

Ⓥ Verse

|D |D/C |G |D |
|D |D/C |G |D |A |A |

Ⓑ Bridge

|C |G |F |A |
|G |D |A |D |A |A |

Ⓒ Chorus

G D	A D	G D	A D
G D	A D	G D	A
D	A	A

The King Shall Return

The night of February 2nd is the traditional night of Imbolc, also known as Candlemas and as Brigit. In fact, this feast probably has more names than any other. It is also the feast about which the least amount of pre-Christian information has survived. The common thread running through all of it is the return or growth of the Light, the return of longer days.

Six weeks after the Winter Solstice we begin to notice that, indeed, the days are growing longer. The promise of warm Summer days is evident, though Winter still remains with us. The modern representation of this feast in the United States is Groundhog Day, whose folklore deals with the length of Winter weather.

If the Goddess is Queen and symbolized by the Moon, then the God is King and His symbol is the Sun. Though night time dominates at this time of year, the King shall return.

The King Shall Return (Imbolc)

words and music by Hugin The Bard

102

The King Shall Return

1. Tho winters grasp still clings to the Earth
   And winter winds blow strong
   The Solstice saw my Lord's holy birth
   Now, Spring it won't be long

2. My Lady tends Her babe while we wait
   Still cloaked in a mantle of white
   Tonight is the night we do celebrate
   The Feast of the waxing light

C. Hail, hail, the King shall return
      My Lord is on His way
   Hail, hail, we look to the Spring
      Today is a longer day

3. So, come ye bards and dancers of olde
   Goods to the feast do bring
   Let the ale flow and tales be told
   We sing the return of the King

(Chorus)

4. Some call it Brigid, Candlemas too
   Flametide and Making New Fire
   Come, all are welcome who worship the Two
   Til daylight we shall not retire

(Chorus)

(The King Shall Return)
4/4 TIME

Ⓥ Verse

| Em | D | G | A B7 |
| Em | D | C B7 | Em A |

Ⓒ Chorus

| A | Em | G A | B7 |
| A | Em | C D | Em A |

    I play this song with a hard driving rhythm. I like to repeat the last line of the chorus a second time and extend the chorus instrumentally by repeating the measure | Em A | three or four times before moving on to the next verse. The repeated measure also works well as an introduction.

Spring Fling

Day and night are of equal length on the Equinox. It is a time of balance. In the Northern Hemisphere, the warm air of Spring has returned to all but the far north. Even there, though it may still snow, the chill is no longer bitter. Fertile life is returning.

Crops are planted. Many animals give birth. Warm breezes through open windows refresh homes long closed to the Winter. There is increased activity everywhere and young hearts turn to love.

This is one of my favorite festivals and not only for the warming and new life, but for the balance. Night and day, Sun and Moon, female and male are all in magickal balance. It is one of the best times for sex magick. Therefore, I have made this a frolic song.

Beware! Any who exhibit sexism at this time do so at their own karmic peril.

Spring Fling

1. Spring, it finally is upon us
   All of life will start anew
   Living gifts all from the Goddess
   Plant yourself a seed or two
      (chorus)

2. Spring, it is a time of rebirth
   All around it's turning green
   They've woken up the sleeping Earth
   Now the Sun is longer seen
      (chorus)

3. Spring, it is a time for plowing
   All that grows is to our gain
   Dig a furrow, seeds go now in
   Pat it down then wait for rain
      (chorus)

4. Spring, it is a time of warming
   Spring, it is a time of cheer
   And we know the children born at
   Winter Solstice started here
      (chorus)

5. Spring, it is a time for laughter
   Spring, it is a time for love
   Sing it out now shake the rafter
   Glory to the Gods above

C. Dance, ye lovely maidens round
   Grab yourself a handsome beau
   And if the couples disappear
   Well, you know how the story goes

(Spring Fling)
4/4 TIME

Ⓥ Verse

|D |G D |D |E⁷ A |
|D |G D |D |A D |D |

Ⓒ Chorus

G	C G	G	A⁷ D
G	C G	G	D G
G	A

This is a delightful song for dancers that tends to go faster with each verse. If the dancers are enjoying themselves, I'll do the song over and over, increasing tempo, until either the dancers or the musicians can't keep up.

Blooming Of The Lady

Perhaps no other Pagan holy day has carried over into mundane life with more persistence than May Day. Even the Atheists of Communism celebrate May 1st as International Workers Day.

Whether one calls it May Day, May Eve or Beltane, it is a time of festival for the entire family. The activity most associated with this festival is the weaving fertility dance around the Maypole. This dance was so much fun that Cromwell banned it when he took power in England and fined the constables five shillings weekly as long as they stood. Many constables gladly paid the fine.

The new growth of Spring is now in bloom. Our Mother, the Earth, is vibrant and alive. This feast, more so than any other, is dedicated to the Goddess. It is the blooming of the Lady.

Blooming of the Lady

1. Tis the blooming of the Lady
     and all her lovely charms
   Yonder comes the Lord now
     to dance within her arms
   Then the Two shall join
     and do the dance of life
   And the Earth shall be reborn again

2. Tis the blooming of the Lady
     such a lovely thing
   Spring is in the air
     it makes you want to sing
   Now she bids us all
     to join the dance of life
   And the Earth shall be reborn again

C. Do the dance of life with us together
   Sing a song of very merry weather
   Do the dance of life with us together
   And the Earth shall be reborn again

3. Tis the blooming of the Lady
     everybody come
   Join us in the circle
     the dancing has begun
   Here we join together
     and do the dance of life
   And the Earth shall be reborn again

(Chorus)

(Blooming of the Lady)
2/4 TIME

Ⓥ Verse

C	Em7	F	G
Am7	Em7	F	G
Am7	Em7	F	G
C	Em7	F	G
C	Em7	F	G

Ⓒ Chorus

C	Em7	F	G
Am7	Em7	F	G
C	Em7	F	G
C	Em7	F	G
C	Em7	F	G

On This Longest Day

The Summer Solstice has long been a time of gathering and festival for all peoples who closely relate to nature. Often this was the largest gathering of the year.

Some groups considered this their New Year and feasting could go on for five or more days. Reunions took place, prospective mates were sought and long Summer days provided pleasant conditions for near round the clock festival.

Another name for Summer Solstice is Midsummer. Many ancient peoples acknowledged only two seasons, Summer and Winter, with the Solstice considered the middle point of each season.

Most ancient megaliths, such as Stonehenge and the Great Pyramid, were aligned so that the rising Sun on Solstice shined in a special way on a particular spot.

On This Longest Day

Intro: Sunrise twixt the standing stones
         On the altar stone today

① Come to the Solstice call with the rising of the Sun
   Here now, it's Midsummer's Day and the festival has begun
   Greetings, my Lady Faire, won't you set your burden down
   Now in the open air we can join the dancers round

[C] Life in the Earth abounds by the Mother and her way
    Drink in the power from my Lord the Sun that's
    On this longest day

② Come to the Solstice dance maybe find yourself a mate
   Here now, it's Midsummer's Day, it's a very important date
   Greetings, my neighbor, now I can see you're looking good
   And I should tell you now, if I found the nerve I would

[C] Life in the Earth abounds by the Mother and her way
    Drink in the power from my Lord, the Sun, that's
    On this longest day

③ Come to the Solstice day and sing a Solstice song
   Here now, it's Midsummer's day as a day it's very long
   Greetings, oh, children too, won't you come along and play
   We can live in glory now as life goes on its way

[C] Life in the Earth abounds by the Mother and her way
    Drink in the power from my Lord the Sun that's
    On this longest day

(On This Longest Day)
       4/4 TIME
Introduction:

|D |C |G |D |

Ⓥ Verse

D	C	G	D
D	C	G	D
D	C	G	D
D	C	G	D	D

Ⓒ Chorus

G	C	G	F
G	C	G	F
C	G	G	D	D

John Barleycorn

The words of this traditional harvest song would seem to be the tale of a most brutal conspiracy and murder, if taken literally. It actually is a joyous analogy of the grain harvest.

Pagans know that all living things share the spark of life, love and consciousness from the Gods. When treated and consumed in a respectful way, that spark becomes one with the new host. Grain becomes the bread of life and survival.

To celebrate the harvest, loaves are sometimes formed in the semblance of a human. This figure later became the Gingerbread Man.

In the spirit of inter-species communication and interaction, the grain and sometimes the bread it became was given a name,
John Barleycorn.

John Barleycorn (Traditional)

John Barleycorn   (Traditional)

There were three men came out of the West
Their fortune for to try
And these three men made a solemn vow
John Barleycorn must die
They rowed, they plowed, they harrowed him in
Threw clods upon his head
And these three men made a solemn oath
John Barleycorn was dead

They left him lie for a very long time
Til the rain from heaven did fall
And little Sir John rose up his head
And so surprised them all
They left him stand til Midsummer's Day
Til he looked both pale and wan
And little Sir John grew a long long beard
And so became a man

They hired men with the sharpened scythe
To cut him at the knee
They rolled him and tied him by the waist
Serving him most laborously
They hired men with sharp pitchforks
To prick him to the heart
But the loader he has served him worse than that
For he's bound him unto a cart

They rode him around and around the field
Til they came unto a barn
And there they swore a cruel oath
On poor John Barleycorn

They hired men with the hickory sticks
To rend him skin from bone
And the miller he has served him worse than that
For he's ground him between two stones

But, little Sir John of the nut brown bowl
And the brandy in his glass
Aye, little Sir John of the nut brown bowl
Proved the strongest man at last
For the huntsman he can't hunt the fox
Nor loudly blow his horn
And the tinker he can't mend either kettle or pots
Wi'out a little John Barleycorn

4/4 TIME

| Dm | Dm | Dm | Dm | (Intro.)

| G | Dm | F C | Dm | (Verse)
G	Dm C	Dm	Dm
G	Dm	F C	Dm
G	Dm C	Dm	Dm
F	C	Dm	Dm
F	G	A	A
G	Dm	F C	Dm
G	Dm C	Dm	Dm

Stand Ye Up For A Boon

Most Neo-Pagans celebrate August 1st as the festival of first harvests. Lughnassad, also called Lammas, translates as "Lugh's Feast". The greatest feast for Lugh in Celtic mythology was for his wedding, greater even than his battle feasts.

In days of olde, family feasts such as weddings and birthdays were treated a bit different than today. Rather than bringing gifts to the couple, the honored ones would give gifts to those in attendance, especially those hearts who had helped their survival. This was sometimes called a granting of the boon. Native Americans have a similar practice called a potlatch or giveaway.

Usually during the feast, one at a time, people would stand to address the couple and ask for things they needed or wanted. If the request were possible to grant and reasonable, it was granted. To deny a reasonable boon was considered an act without honor.

To understand the importance of reasonable boons, read the story of Rhiannon and Pwyll in the Welsh Mabinogion and remember to stand ye up for a boon.

Stand Ye Up For A Boon

1. Hot days in Summer, come walk or come run
   For the wedding is special today
   Here at the wedding we've flowers for bedding
   The two getting married today

1st C. And it's Hey! Stand ye up for a boon
   For this is a wedding of olde
   And it's Hey! Within reason it's granted
   And now let the tales be told

2. Beautiful lady, you carry a baby
   Of promise inside of your womb
   Here comes the Lord with his most holy sword
   Tis a sign that the harvest is soon

2nd C. And it's Hey! Stand ye up for a boon
   If ye be neighbor or kin
   And it's Hey! Within reason it's granted
   And now let the dancing begin

3. Hot days in Summer, the Winter is slumbering
   Off in a world far away
   Although not the longest, this day is the strongest
   Of everything Summer can say

3rd C. And it's Hey! Stand ye up for a boon
   Sing it on out like a choir
   And it's Hey! Within reason it's granted
   And now let the couple retire

(Stand Ye Up For A Boon)

Ⓥ Verse

D	C	G	D
C	G	D	D
D	C	G	D
C	G	D	D

© Chorus

C	C	G	D
C	G	D	D
C	C	G	D
C	G	D	D

Autumn Again

Autumn Equinox is a time of celebrating the harvest and the other time of magickal balance. The Sun rides lower in the sky and day and night are of equal length. The feast at this time often had the most variety of the year with samples from the entire harvest.

People could tell if it would be a lean winter by the size of the harvest and the weather was still mild. This made it a time of looking both to the future and to the past.

Some say the God leaves us at this time to live in the land of the dead until Yule or even Vernal Equinox. But, this is a God we are talking about and certainly not a forgotten one. Whichever mythos one chooses, we know He doesn't really die.

Autumn Again

(1) Leaves in color come a'tumbling down
 I hope to have your loving when you come around
 Because the harvest is in now there's joy to be found
 Before winter winds blow again

(2) See the table laid with acorns and grain
 All the fruits of the harvest, no two are the same
 They say the barley is good for making ale again
 So, I can drink to your health, my friend

(C) The Lord is low in the western sky
 Although we know he doesn't really die
 The Lord will rule from the other side
 Til he starts returning again

(3) Bring the cauldron and the sacred wood
 It's time to worship as you know we should
 For the Gods bring forth and their bounty is good
 Ah, here tis Autumn again

(4) The time has come, my Lord will go away
 Ah, but don't be sad, this is part of his way
 He gives his power to the Lady and in this way he stays
 While we dance the circle again

(Chorus)

(5) Leaves in color come a'tumbling down
 I hope to have your loving when you come around
 Because the harvest is in now there's joy to be found
 Before winter winds blow again

(Autumn Again)
2/4 TIME

Ⓥ Verse

G	G/F#	Em7	D	
C	G/B	Am7	D	
G	G/F#	Em7	D	
C	D	G	D	

Ⓒ Chorus

G	G/F#	Em7	D	
C	G/B	Am7	D	
G	G/F#	Em7	D	
C	D	G	D	

This is an instrumental line that can be used between chorus and verse and between two verses

| C | D | G | G | |

Dark Night

Contemporary society celebrates Halloween or All Hallows Eve with a night of revelry and often with ghoulish costumes.

In the olde days, you had better be finished with harvest, for winter weather is upon us. Survival had become a serious business. Animal stocks were thinned at this time to conserve feed grains. Some of what was not salted and dried for Winter would likely show up at this feast.

To some, a time of chaos and misrule began tonight to last until Yule. To others, this was the new year and a "Dumb Supper" or "Feast of the Dead" was made to share with friends and ancestors no longer living.

The veil between the living and the dead is never so easily crossed as it is this night. Good reason to be apprehensive for those who don't understand. For tonight the veil is very thin.

Dark Night

1. Tonight the veil is very thin
   Our ancient kin we shall let in
   To feast and play a while with us
   And use our bodies. Do you trust ~ Samhain?

2. Dark of night is growing long
   Winter winds are blowing strong
   My Lord has gone away to rule
   The other side. Dark shining jewel ~ Samhain

C. Dark night in Autumn souls on the wind
   My loving ancestors I call in
   To share in the riches of this other side
   Stay while we worship and then on the wind do ride

3. Souls upon the wind do ride
   Both good and bad from the other side
   Take care to keep your mortal mind
   Or on your own soul they may dine ~ Samhain

4. Now the hour is growing late
   Circle Master guard the gate
   Let the good souls in to play
   Banish evil far away ~ Samhain

(Chorus)

5. Mother Goddess you say when
   By your love we live again
   Til we die our Lord does wait
   So, tonight we celebrate Samhain

(Chorus)

(Dark Night)
4/4 time

Ⓥ Verse

E^{m7}	D	C	E^{m7}
E^{m7}	D	C	E^{m7}
C	C	B^{m7}	B^{m7}
C	C	B^7	B^7	E^{m7}

Ⓒ Chorus

E^{m7}	G	A	E^{m7}
E^{m7}	G	A	E^{m7}
D	C	E^{m7}	E^{m7}
D	C	A	A	A	E^{m7}

Repeat the last E^{m7} of both Verse and Chorus until you're ready to move on, usually eight times.

I play this song at a fast tempo. It can be both fun and spooky with lots of witchy cackling and laughter on the breaks.

Commonly pronounced Samhain (sah-wen), I use modern Irish and say Samhain (sam-hane).

As we complete our musical journey 'round the Wheel of the Year, we find ourselves once again at the Winter Solstice. The weather keeps most of us inside now.

It is a good time to study and reflect or to make those craft items which are so time consuming to make. Before electronic media, it was a time of telling the tales, myths and cosmology of the people, often by the light of a warm and meditative fire.

Time seems to go slowly during the long darkness of night. It is a time of dangerous cold and of awesome beauty.

A December Full Moon is a sight to behold. The Moon is now the closest it ever gets to the Earth, making it the largest of the year. It also rides higher in the sky than at any other time.

So too, at this time of year, is the Earth closer to the Sun than it is in June. Yet, in the North of our world, it is winter.

These phenomena can help remind us that all thing are relative and all things change. No single moment is the same as the next. Each one is unique unto itself. Yet, everything is intimately connected with that which came before and with that which will follow.

Long cold nights of winter hold within them the promise of longer and warmer days to come. All creatures are aware of these changes in our yearly cycle and follow them as part of the natural process.

The forces which propel our tiny star system through the heavens are indeed quite awesome, spectacular and wonderful, if at times a bit frightening. The life zone covering our tiny sphere can be compared to the fragile skin of an onion, while the vast distances between stars are almost beyond comprehension. So, instead of worrying about how small we are compared to the universe, we celebrate things like good weather and harvests, things that are easily understood.

Acts of celebrating cycles of nature help bring us in tune with our world and the rest of cosmic creation. They open us up to our life force within, which is itself a direct channel to the force of creation. The joyous times of feasting the wheel are truly sacred acts.

While the Gods infuse the sacred frenzy of a high day circle dance, the dance is a reflection of the other side of our activity cycle; the time of withdrawal and meditation when we might ponder imponderables and touch all the vastness of creation by journeying within.

Drifting Through Time

1. Sailing the universe
   And drifting through time
   Hailing what some would curse
   Or call it a crime

2. Turning with the Earth
   And all those on board
   Yearning for each rebirth
   Each note of the chord

C. Each song of Spring I hear
   Each song, each year
   Renews my life again
   There is no end

3. Laughing at childs play
   Such joy does it give
   Having another day
   To learn how to live

4. Finding our separate ways
   Like bees to the hive
   Binding our destiny
   With each of our lives

   (Chorus)

   Sailing the universe
   And drifting through time

(Drifting Through Time)
4/4 TIME

Ⓥ Verse

A△	A△	C△	C△
G	D	A△	A△
A△	A△	C△	C△
G	D	E	E

ⓒ Chorus

D	C#m	F#m	Bm
C△	C#m	D	E
D	C#m	F#m	Bm
G	C△	F	E

138

Ah, the Dancer's Band!
I started writing this song on the way home from work one day. The words and music all came together in about three hours time. Tis a bit of a boisterous tune which can raise the pitch of a party to near frenzy.

I dedicate this song to all those who delight in active dance as a form of feast and worship.

The Dancers Band

words and music by Hugin The Bard

The Dancer's Band

C) We feast, we feast, we feast and then we dance.
   We gather here to worship, then we feast and then we dance

1) Myrddin had a fiddle that he played upon his chin
   And the music that he made invited dancers to come in
   With a song within his heart and a song within his hand
   And the dancers all delighted when he joined in the band

(Chorus)

2) Myfanwy for a birthday got a boudhrain for a gift
   And she learned to play that boudhrain not a rhythm beat she missed
   Whether beat to tap your toe or a waltz across the land
   And the dancers all delighted when she joined in the band

(Chorus)

3) Donald had a mandolin he played upon his knee
   And he played those many strings inviting dancers liberty
   He played magick in his heart with the magick in his hand
   And the dancers all delighted when he joined in the band

(Chorus)

4) Molly had a pennywhistle, into it she would blow
   And the notes that she would play inspired dancers round to go
   She played high up in the air, she played low unto the land
   And the dancers all delighted when she joined in the band

(Chorus)

(The Dancers Band)
    4/4 TIME

C Chorus

| Dm | Dm | Dm | C |
| Dm | Dm | F Dm C | Dm |

V Verse

Dm	C	Dm	Dm
F	C	A	A
Dm	Dm	F	C
Dm	Dm	F C	Dm

Aye of Newt

newt \ˈn(y)üt\ n. [by syllabic merging] any of various small salamanders that can live both on land and in water.

Newts have gotten a bad rap from Will Shakespeare on. The Bard-on-Avon put forth that witches had a penchant for using their tiny eyeballs as a prime ingredient in cauldron brews.

Come on! It would take at least a hundred of the little critters to heap a teaspoon with their eyes. And only the most dextrous could isolate those optic items.

So, let's play on the words. Not "Eye of Newt" for an evil brew, but "Aye of Newt" for an honorable good time of living with both eyes right where they belong, in the newt.

"Aye" is an affirmative, often meaning "yes" or "O.K.". Aye, we'll sing. Aye, we'll dance. Aye, aye, Captain, we'll make a grand time of it.

Haul Away Home

A Bard's qualifying function is to tell the sacred tales in song. Yet, a Bard must also be ready to entertain. The sacred messages of life can sometimes be a burden to the weary. Mundane songs with a bit of humor can lighten the burden.

Haul Away Home is a mundane tale of a sea voyage around the world. It can be enjoyed for the tale itself, and brings many a self-proclaimed "non-singer" to sing out with the chorus. A jolly good tale of a journey.

The initiated know that every journey brings growth and knowledge, if not truly a transformation. The surface belief of relaxed obligation to deep thoughts and meaning is what lightens the burden. Relaxation allows the symbols of this simple song to penetrate deep and bring with them other lessons which might otherwise have been missed.

Fun is Good!

Haul Away Home

words and music by Hugin The Bard

Chorus

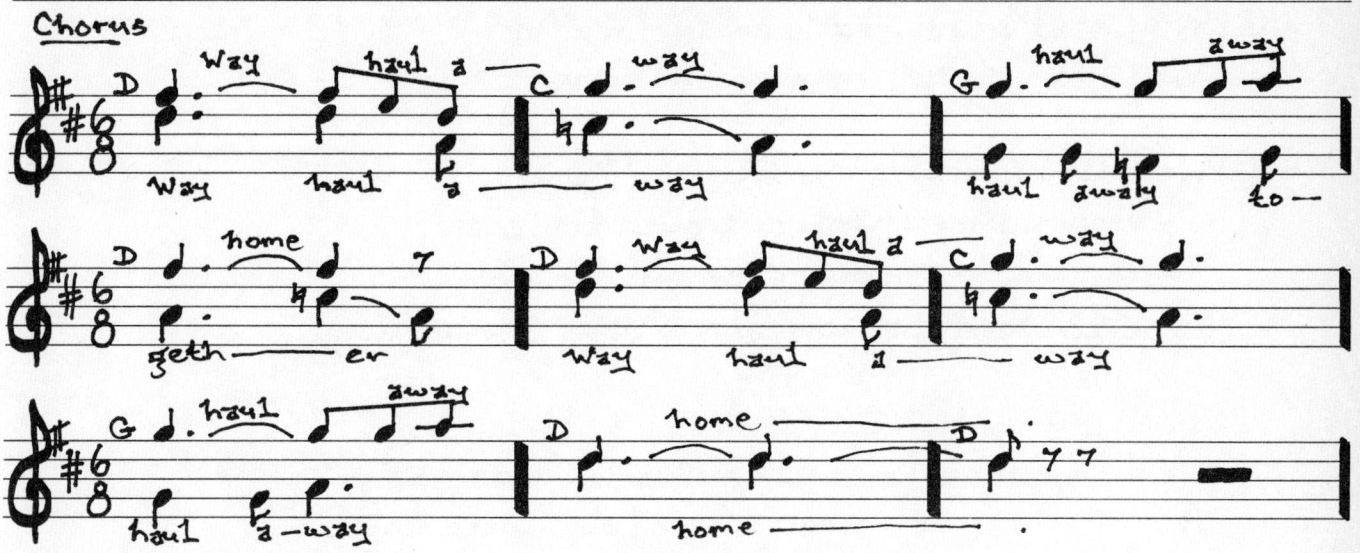

Note: Chorus is written an octave higher than actually sung.

Verse

1. We sailed from Nantucket in seventy-three to escort a merchant out o-ver the sea. 'Twas lost in a storm over old Tripol-i and the song that we sang it was Haul a-way

Haul Away Home

[C] Way haul away, haul away together
   Way haul away, haul away home

(1) We sailed from Nantucket in '73
   To escort a merchant out over the sea
   Twas lost in a storm over old Tripoli
   And the song that we sang it was Haul Away

(2) Then out through Gibralter round Africa bold
   We rounded the Horn and the Winter was cold
   Across the great ocean where tales were told
   And the song that we sang it was Haul Away

(3) Round islands and spices and magickal trees
   To river of Tigers in Persia to please
   Then out with the tide and the southerly seas
   And the song that we sang it was Haul Away

(4) The day it was bright on the Cape of Good Hope
   Where I fell in the sea, but they got me a rope
   The Captain had news, going home to elope
   And the song that we sang it was Haul Away

(5) Then back to Nantucket where English is spoke
   The crew all got drunk and then tossed in the poke
   And after a month don't you know we're all broke
   And the song that we sang it was Haul Away

(Haul Away Home)
6/8 TIME

C Chorus

| D | C | G | D | |
| D | C | G | D | D |

V. Verse

D	C	G	D	
D	C	D	C	
A	D			

Cosmick Cowboy

The New Age is a concept from the western world. One of the western world's most colorful characters is the freedom loving Cowboy of North America. I have attempted to merge these two themes in this one song. It's a New Age tune like no other.

From the outer space exploring culture of the western world comes that range riding Town Crier of the Aquarian Age....
The Cosmick Cowboy!

Cosmick Cowboy

1) I just want to be a Cosmick Cowboy
From Andromeda unto the Milky Way
If you don't like me to be a Cosmick Cowboy
You can leave or wait until I go away
And I won't stay here cox I'm always moving
Yes, I'm always on my way

2) If you think that you're a Cosmick Cowboy
You might ask yourself a question on the way
If I'm gonna be a Cosmick Cowboy
Will I have my home in yesterday?
And I can't stay here cox I'm always thinking
That I'm always on my way

3) If you hang on to a Cosmick Cowboy
He might read your palm or read your stars away
But, when you hang on to a Cosmick Cowboy
You'll be moving if you hang on for a day
And I don't stay here cox I'm always reading
That I'm always on my way

4) You know I'm gonna be a Cosmick Cowboy
Gonna be a Cosmick Cowboy all my day
And I know I'm gonna be a Cosmick Cowboy
Til the questions of my life have gone away
And I won't stay here cox I'm always learning
That I'm always on my way

(Cosmick Cowboy)
4/4 TIME

Ⓥ Verse

G	G7	C	C
D	D	G	D
G	G7	C	C
D	D	G	G
C	G	C	D	D

Northern Meadow

There once was a time when lovers could safely meet in the woods for that most sacred of unions. Communion within the natural world provided an environment conducive to the raising of mortal love and pleasure to a truly spiritual level. Our concept of romantic love was greatly shaped by those emotional and spiritual bondings.

Most land is privately owned today. Stripped, manicured and domesticated. Our towns and cities have grown to cover vast areas and trysts upon public land entails serious risk of legal and social prosecution.

Yet, as long as it is possible to escape the fetters of our cities and social conventions, even if only briefly, it is possible for romantic love to exist and grow.

Thankfully, some wilderness areas remain where the pure love of the Goddess and God can still be practiced. And practice makes perfect.

Northern Meadow

① In the northern meadow just a league away from town
You know the meadow with the oak trees around
There's a place in the meadow that to me is hallowed ground
Where the first time my lover lay me down

② It was springtime in the meadow during planting of the corn
When we walked from the fields then we stepped around the thorn
Til we came to the meadow where a deer had shed his horn
In that place our love was truly born

③ Now, that place in the meadow it was fragrant, it was sweet
It was soft as a downy pillow lain upon your feet
And the flowers in the meadow all in bloom were such a treat
Then we kissed and our inner souls did meet

(Chorus)

④ It was late in the meadow there were stars up above
When we kissed once again and my heart sang like a dove
Then we walked from the meadow and we found that thereof
We were blind to the darkness by our love

⑤ Now we're old and the meadow isn't quite so far from town
You know the meadow with some oak trees around
There's a place in the meadow to our child is hallowed ground
Where the first time with lover they lay down

C In the northern meadow there's a spot of hallowed ground
In the northern meadow with the oak trees around

Exit: In the northern meadow there's a spot of hallowed ground
Where the first time my lover lay me down

(Northern Meadow)
4/4 Time

Ⓥ Verse

D	D/C	G	D
D	D/C	Em7	A
D	D/C	G	D
D	D/C	D	D

Ⓒ Chorus

| F#m | Bm | G | D |
| F#m | Bm | G | A |

Exit

| D | D/C | G | D |
| D | D/C | D Dsus4 | D |

A Turtle Island Song

Turtle Island is the most common and recognized name for North America by Native Americans.

This becomes not just a dancing song, but a sacred song when the spiritual nature of the land and its true name is acknowledged. For then, the dancing does not take place so much on the land as it does within the loving bosom of our Mother, the Earth.

Won't you dance with me,
    beautiful darlin' ?

A Turtle Island Song

1. Won't you dance with me on Turtle Island
   Won't you dance with me on Turtle Isle
   Won't you dance with me under the moonlight
   Underneath the stars above
   Won't you dance with me on Turtle Island
   Won't you dance with me on Turtle Isle

2. Won't you dance with me, beautiful darlin'
   Won't you dance with me here for a while
   Won't you dance with me under the sunshine
   Underneath the sky above
   Won't you dance with me, beautiful darlin'
   Won't you dance with me here for a while

3. Won't you dance with me on Turtle Island
   Won't you dance with me on Turtle Isle
   Won't you dance with me under the moonlight
   Underneath the stars above
   Won't you dance with me on Turtle Island
   Won't you dance with me on Turtle Isle

(Exit)
   Won't you dance with me, beautiful darlin'
   Won't you dance with me on Turtle Isle

(A Turtle Island Song)
   4/4 TIME

Ⓥ Verse

E	E	A	A
E	E	B7	B7
E	E	A	A
E	B7	E	E
A	A	E	E
D	G	C	B7
E	E	A	A
E	B7	E	E

Note: First two lyric lines of each verse repeat.

160

Wandering Minstrel

Before Electronic Media (B.E.M.), the traveling musician was quite welcome in small rural communities. Living rather simply, they traveled mostly on foot and performed for little more than room and board. It was also not uncommon for them to be adept at such things as juggling and slight of hand tricks.

News of events, fashion and politics were only part of what these itinerant singers carried. In providing entertainment, it can be said, they linked together the separate places of the culture. A song written in one place might be taken up by others who then might send a change of fashion to be taken up in return.

In this context, they were the bearers of the living culture and the strands of the web of the people.

Wandering Minstrel
words and music by Hugin The Bard

Wandering Minstrel

(1) Wand'ring minstrel sing a song
   For the folk at the feast and the fair
   Wand'ring minstrel sing a song
   For the love of the light and the air

(2) Wand'ring minstrel tell a tale
   Of the folk and their life desire
   Wand'ring minstrel tell a tale
   Of the hot and the cold of the fire

(3) Wand'ring minstrel do a ditty
   For the babe and the son and the daughter
   Wand'ring minstrel do a ditty
   For the bread and the wine and the water

(4) Wand'ring minstrel play a part
   Of the play of the miracle birth
   Wand'ring minstrel play a part
   Of the song of the life of the Earth

(5) Wand'ring minstrel lead a dance
   Sing it out so that all can hear it
   Wand'ring minstrel lead a dance
   Sing it out of life and spirit

(Wandering Minstrel)
4/4 TIME

Ⓥ Verse

D	D	G	D
A	A	D	D
D	D	G	D
A	A	D	D
G	D	A	D
G	D	A	D

One day I was talking with Carl Weschcke of Llewellyn Publications about dream lovers and soul mates. He suggested I write a song, "Something like, I left my true heart out on the astral plane". This song is the result of that suggestion. Thank you, Carl. Blessed Be!

Love On The Astral Plane

words and music by Hugin The Bard

1. Used to be that life was just a daily sort of grind, strugglin' every day just to sur— vive. Then one night I made the most ex-traor-di-nar—y find. Like a

165

Love On The Astral Plane

1. Used to be that life was just
   A daily sort of grind
   Strugglin' every day just to survive
   Then one night I made
   The most extraordinary find
   Like a flower in my heart, love is alive

2. I told my friends about it
   And they thought it was a curse
   They said it only happened in my dreams
   But, the changes in my life
   Are much better than for worse
   It's even more than it seems

C. I found love on the Astral Plane
   My life will never be the same
   My heart's no longer in pain
   Since I found love on the Astral Plane

3. Now that I have found you
   And I know that love is real
   I hope that I can find you in the light
   Though, I love you heart and soul
   Then your body I could feel
   We could love all day and all night

C. I found love on the Astral Plane
   My life will never be the same
   My heart's no longer in pain
   Since I found love on the Astral Plane

(Love On The Astral Plane)
   4/4 TIME

Ⓥ Verse

D	C	G	D
G	C	D	D
D	C	G	D
G	C	A	A

Ⓒ Chorus

D	G	D	D
F#m	Bm	G	A
D	G	D	Bm
Em	A	D	C
G	D

Tarry On

To tarry is to remain or be delayed in a place.

Tarry On was written with the intent to be used in the preparation of an area for sacred use. While it stops short of actually casting a magick circle, it does address each of the seven sacred directions.

If so used, the directional energies do attend, or tarry on, and we have an area well balanced in three dimensions. More than three dimensions are in use if a circle is properly cast.

I have had good results with this song as an energy raising dance of the assembly while the High Priesthood does circle casting within the ring of dancers. It has also been popular during the feast.

Tarry On

words and music by Hugin The Bard

Verses: 1, 2, 4, 6, 8

Verses: 3, 5, 7, 9

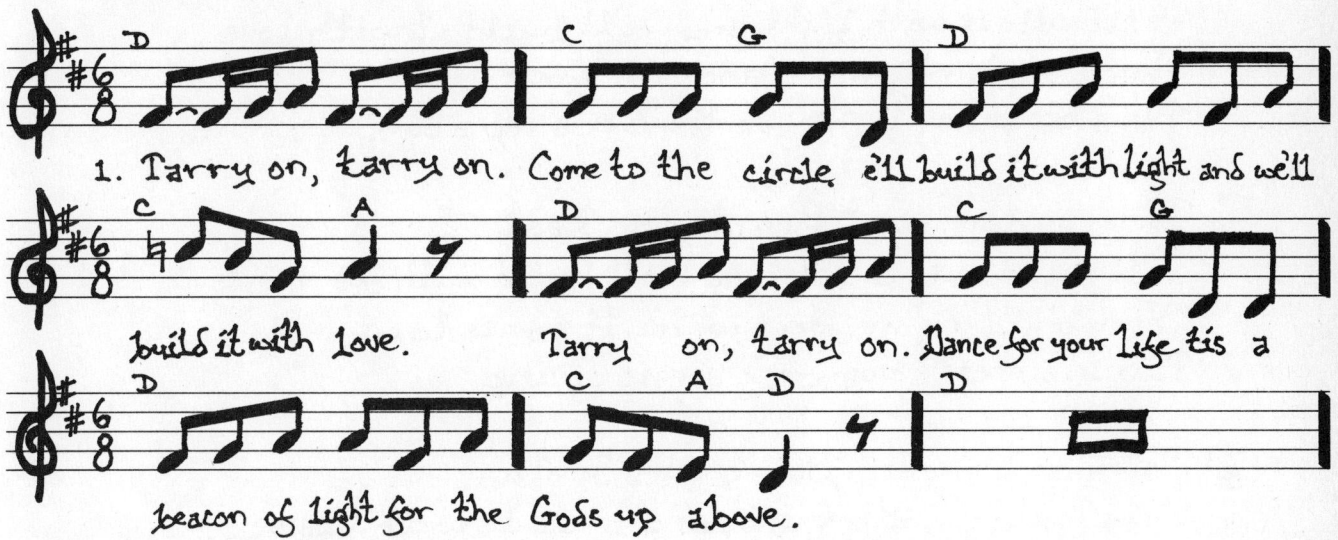

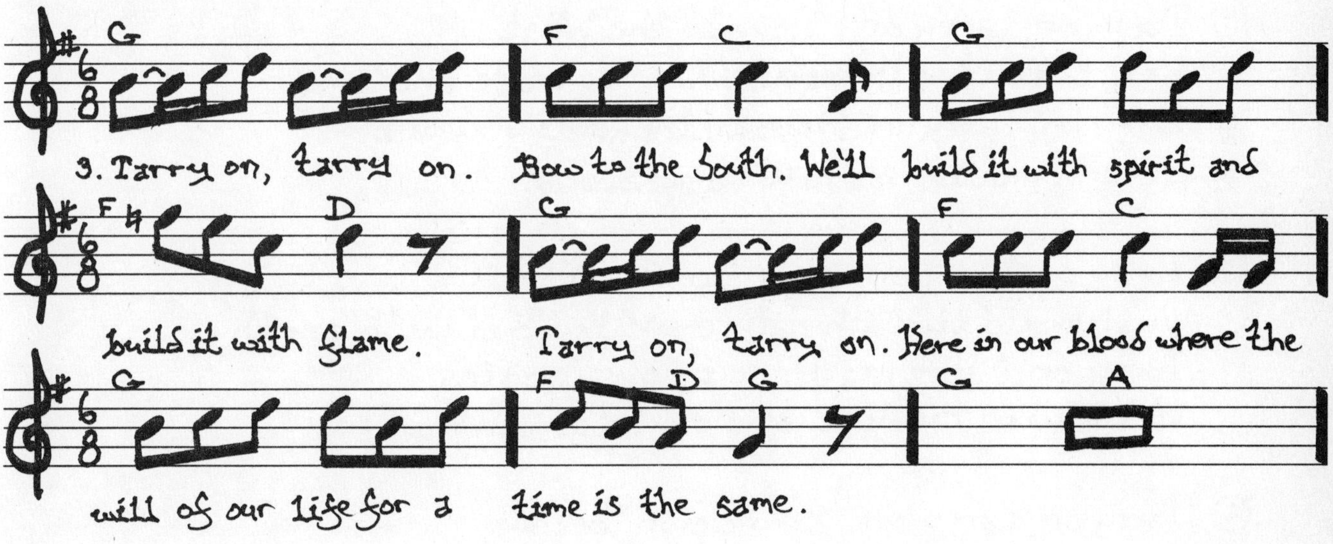

Tarry On

1. Tarry on, tarry on, Come to the circle
   We'll build it with light and we'll build it with love
   Tarry on, tarry on, Dance for your life
   Tis a beacon of light for the Gods up above

2. Tarry on, tarry on, Bow to the East
   We'll build with the air and we'll build with our minds
   Tarry on, tarry on, Here where it comes to us
   Take in a breath now, the air is divine

3. Tarry on, tarry on, Bow to the South
   We'll build it with spirit and build it with flame
   Tarry on, tarry on, Here in our blood
   Where the will of our life for a time is the same

4. Tarry on, tarry on, Bow to the West
   We'll build it with feelings and courage and song
   Tarry on, tarry on, Here in the fertile womb
   Ocean emotion has now come along

5. Tarry on, tarry on, Bow to the North
   We'll build it with nature and build it with earth
   Tarry on, tarry on, Here in our bodies
   We grow in the field and mountain in mirth

6. Tarry on, tarry on, Bow down below
   Sing to the Goddess, our Mother we call
   Tarry on, tarry on, Lady in White
   You are dear to our hearts for your babes we are all

⑦ Tarry on, tarry on, Bow up above
   To the God in the Sky, to the God in the Wood
   Tarry on, tarry on, My Lord in Red
   Has come to the circle, His presence is good

⑧ Tarry on, tarry on, Bow to the center
   You bow to yourself when you're balanced inside
   Tarry on, tarry on, Welcome the Oneness
   Our circle's the same as the Universe wide

⑨ Tarry on, tarry on, Come to the circle
   We've built it with light and we've built it with love
   Tarry on, tarry on, Dance for your life
   Tis a beacon of light for the Gods up above.

   Grounding, grounding, grounding

(Tarry On)
   6/8 TIME
Verses: 1, 2, 4, 6, 8

| D | C G | D | C A | |
| D | C G | D | C-A D | D |

Verses: 3, 5, 7, 9

| G | F C | G | F D | |
| G | F C | G | F-D G | A |

The Fey, They Come

In a meadow by the banks of one of America's most pristine rivers was this next song composed. My daughter, Ami, was with me that warm summer evening. We had a small campfire.

As dusk turned to dark, the structure of the music became clear. Over and over the verse was played. We both sang the melody, words as yet unknown.

Gradually, the meadow became active. The smallest of the nature spirits began a circular dance, to be joined by their larger cousins. A few were as big as a small house.

Phrases were contributed, one by one, as the Fey let us know what the words would be.

The meadow glowed with other-worldly life long after we retired to happy and wondrous dreams.

The Fey, They Come

words and music by Hugin The Bard

The Fey, They Come

1. Hey Hum, the Fey, they come
   O'er the hill down dale
   Hey ring, the Fey, they sing
   And they tell a tale
   Hey prance, the Fey, they dance
   Let not the music fail
   Hey Hum, the Fey, they come
   Join us in the vale

2. Hey Hum, the Fey, they come
   Led by King and Queen
   Hey press, the Fey, they dress
   Like you've never seen
   Hey Hee, their finery
   To some is thought obscene
   Hey Hum, the Fey, they come
   Join us in the green

3. Hey Hum, the Fey, they come
   To the mortal plane
   Hey feast, when this you eat
   You'll never be the same
   Hey Ho, the Fey, they go
   Round and round again
   Hey Hum, the Fey, they come
   Join us in our game

(The Fey, They Come)
4/4 TIME

(v.) Verse

A	G	D	A
A	G	D	A
D	E	A	D
A	G	D	A

Since Last Time

Reincarnation is an intriguing theory to some. To others, it is a certainty, it is reality. If reincarnation is a fact, what happens between lives and why don't more people remember past lives?

Ask these questions of people and you will receive a multitude of answers and opinions. It is not the type of thing easily documented by scientific method.

Some say that we choose many of the conditions into which we are reborn. Our parents and loved ones, the location and time of our birth are but some of those choices.

If spiritual evolution toward union with the Oneness is the real meaning of life, these choices take on great importance.

How then are these decisions made? I, for one, hope there will be some help in deciding when to be reborn again.

Since Last Time

1. I am a spirit wandering
Upon the veil of time
Between the realms of night and day
Between the lines of rhyme
Come talk with me and sit a while
Help me to decide
When to be reborn again
Since last time I have died

2. Tell me, do the flowers bloom
In springtime any more?
And do the winter's howling winds
Still blow beneath the door?
Is summertime still hot and bright?
Is the ocean wide?
And autumn colors I recall
Since last time I have died

3. Children used to laugh and play
With anything in sight
Married ones would make their love
And married ones would fight
Gods and nations went to war
Swollen with their pride
Or is the world a freer place
Since last time I have died

④ I am a spirit wandering
Upon the veil of time
Between the realms of night and day
Between the lines of rhyme
Come talk with me and sit a while
Help me to decide
When to be reborn again
Since last time I have died

(Since Last Time)
    4/4 TIME
Ⓥ Verse

|Dm C |Bm9 Bb |Bb A |Dm |

|Dm C |Bm9 Bb |Bb A |Dm |Dm |

|F |C |Bb |Bb |

|F |C |Bb Asus4 A|Dm |Dm |

The Messenger

Often, a messenger will go around to celebrants to inform or remind them of a meeting time and place. Usually, the messenger is a human assigned to the task. Sometimes it is other.

When the mundane and magickal worlds meet, our senses can be altered along with our perceptions. We may not recognize the messenger as such. If not, perhaps we are not properly prepared. Of course, the Messenger of the Gods can appear at any time in any form. It is to one's benefit to recognize and hear the message.

Then again, maybe these lyrics are fanciful symbols of normal events. The plate upon the shelf could be a large flat rock at the top of a long hill or bluff, or maybe . . . .

The Messenger

1. It was early in the morning then
   As I began me day
   I thought that I heard talking
   And I thought that I heard say
   That Hu Gadarn, the Messenger,
   Around to me would come
   Then I was reminded
   Of the pounding of the drum

2. He was kind of like a Leprechaun
   Not graceful like an elf
   But, he danced a jolly jig
   Upon the plate upon the shelf
   And he asked me to remind you
   That before tomorrow comes
   We will meet and dance together
   At the pounding of the drum

3. I scarcely did believe
   That I beheld what I had done
   A flashing of an instant
   And the little one was gone
   An instant more I found meself
   Where everyone had come
   And the Moon was rising
   With the pounding of the drum

④ It was early in the morning then
   As I began me day
   I thought that I heard talking
   And I thought that I heard say
   That Hu Gadarn, the Messenger
   Around to me would come
   Then I was reminded
   As the pounding of the drum

Note: Last two lines of each verse repeat

(The Messenger)
    4/4 TIME

Ⓥ Verse

D	G D	G D	Em7 A
D	G D	G D	Em7 A D
G D	Em7 A D	D	D

<u>Dance With Me Darlin'</u>

Strained is the heart that loves one far away. But, the High Day comes and people journey to gather once again. Bonds of spirit and community are strengthened by the activities of journey, worship and feasting. Friendships get renewed, lovers meet and part and the spirit is nourished.

Late in the feast, some go off to sleep or love. Others may begin the journey home. Then, who can blame the strained of heart for wanting to prolong the moment of holding their lover in their arms, to dance just one more song?

Dance With Me Darlin'

[C.] Dance with me darlin'
Don't say adieu
Hear that I love you
For honest I do
Dance with me darlin'
Don't say good night
Drink of my true love
Til mornin' brings light

(1) Living our lives apart
Seeing you now and then
Always you're in my heart
Dance with me once again

(Chorus)

(2) After the feast is done
After the bread and wine
After the games and song
Dance with me one more time

(Chorus)

(3) I want to be near your charms
I wanted you all night long
Now that you're in my arms
Dance with me one more song

(Chorus)

(Dance With Me Darlin')
       3/4 TIME

C Chorus

D	F#m	G	D
G	D	Em7	A
G	D	F#m	G
G	D	G A	D

V Verse

F#m	G	D	D
G	A	D	D
Bm	G	D	D
D	A	D	D

They Call Us Witches

Until recently, for many generations have Wiccans been subject to persecution and disinformation. Sometimes more so, thankfully, a little less these days as we move into the Aquarian Age.

It is safe enough now, in most places, to openly put forth the ideas and ways of life which have kept Wicca alive in the hearts of Her followers through all this time. May this next song do just that.

Some have called this song a Wiccan anthem. It is not my place to declare it as such. For that to be, many Wiccans would have to take the song to heart teaching it to others as part of their living traditions.

While this could happen, it was not my compositional intent. I merely meant it to be a good song.

Like our Gods, we are love!

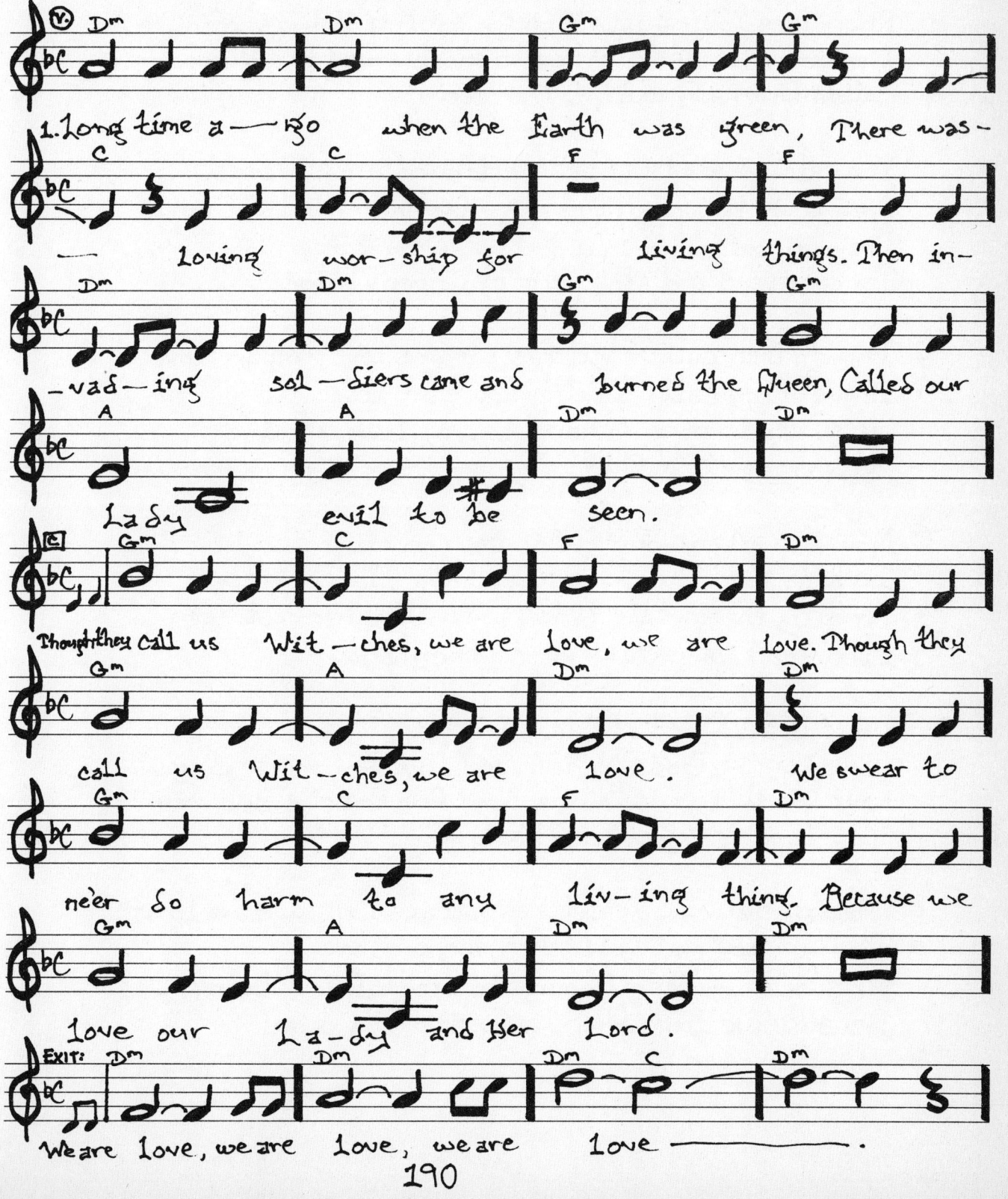

They Call Us Witches

① Long time ago when the Earth was green
   There was loving worship for living things
   Then invading soldiers came and burned the Queen
   Called Our Lady evil to be seen

② They stole our places and destroyed our shrines
   They took the Holy Names and made them saints divine
   They cursed our holy worship every time
   Tortured us and stole our children's minds

© Though they call us Witches, we are love, we are love
   Though they call us Witches, we are love
   We swear to ne'er do harm to any living thing
   Because we love Our Lady and Her Lord

③ Now we plant our fields row on row
   Invoke the Sun on high and the Earth below
   And by the fertile Moon we will a harvest sow
   And teach our children so they know

④ Love is all Our Lady asks in due
   Love for the Gods on high and love for me and you
   Love for all living things, love for the old and new
   Yes, love, so you see it's true

© Though they call us Witches, we are love, we are love
   Though they call us Witches, we are love
   We swear to ne'er do harm to any living thing
   Because we love Our Lady and Her Lord

5. Though death may come and take our lives away
We have no fear of death. Tis Our Lady's way
We'll be reborn again to love another day
And learn! This is why we say

C. Though they call us Witches, we are love, we are love
Though they call us Witches, we are love
We swear to ne'er do harm to any living thing
Because we love Our Lady and Her Lord

Exit: We are love, We are love, We are love!

(They Call Us Witches)
4/4 TIME

V. Verse

Dm	Dm	Gm	Gm
C	C	F	F
Dm	Dm	Gm	Gm
A	A	Dm	Dm

C. Chorus

Gm	C	F	Dm
Gm	A	Dm	Dm
Gm	C	F	Dm
Gm	A	Dm	Dm

Exit:

| Dm | Dm | Dm C | Dm |

Within The Well

More than water
   To refresh
Is contained
   Within the well

To be discovered
   In the depths
Are mysteries
   Within the well

The spirit of
   A Lady dwells
And there protects
   Within the well

A nymph, a sylph
   A sweet undine
A Goddess Muse
   Within the well

Greenwood Down

Tis well met in worship which takes place in the natural environment to address and seek the approval of those nature spirits who reside at the chosen location or nearby.

After receiving the sanction of local entities, it is then appropriate to cleanse, purify and in your own way prepare the area for sacred rite. Please do not damage or relocate anything other than dry brush in the area without its permission. Any human litter should of course be removed.

Ever remember that your way of worship is a private matter between yourself and the Gods. Those not in attendance need no memory of your worship and must commune with Diety in their own way.

"And it harm none
   Do what thou will"

Greenwood Down

words and music by Hugin The Bard

Greenwood Down

[C] On Greenwood Down we dance around
    'Neath the pale moonlight
    'Round a fire prayer goes higher
    On a sacred night

1. Oh, spirits near, I call ye here
    Here, wherein ye dwell
    To ask permission for our mission
    Worship here to tell

(Chorus)

2. East and South and West and North
    Up and down, inside
    Into the middle there's a riddle
    In the circle wide

(Chorus)

3. With She and He, you and me
    Do wonders in the air
    A magick spell, but not to tell
    To those who were not there

(Chorus)

4. We'll unite in sacred rite
    Near the brake and fen
    Meeting merry, parting merry
    Merry meet again

(Chorus)

Greenwood Down
6/8 TIME

©. Chorus

| Dm | G | Dm C | Dm |
| Dm | G | Dm C | Dm |

Ⓥ. Verse

| G | Dm | F C | A |
| G | Dm | F C | Dm |

(Instrument)

| C | Dm | Dm | Dm |
| C | Dm | Dm |

"To sleep, perchance to dream."
(Shakespeare)

<u>Maidens and Wizards and Fools</u>

Dreams have been an important part of life as long as there has been life to dream. The girl in satin and bows goes through a rather full experience of dreams.

She begins with having her dreams shaped by the stories of another and by acting out those dreams in the waking state. Eventually, her conscious mind goes completely over to the dream life she has created.

Whether she has gone on to a different plane of existence or merely left the village to pursue her dreams, we are left guessing.

Maidens and Wizards and Fools

words and music by Hugin The Bard

1: There once was a girl dressed in satin and bows, And what she would do, Lord on-ly knows. Down by the river in the pale morning light, Living her dreams of the night.

C: Now, dream a sweet dream or dream of lust. Dream for-ever, for dream you must. Or dream a terror and live your dream, And dream your life a-way.

Maidens and Wizards and Fools

① There once was a girl dressed in satin and bows
And what she would do, Lord only knows
Down by the river in the pale morning light
Living her dreams of the night

② She longed for the boy dressed in denim and gold
And relished a life in the tales that he told
Of large charging stallions and castles and jewels
And maidens and wizards and fools

[C] Now, dream a sweet dream or dream of lust
Dream forever, for dream you must
Or dream a terror and live your dream
And dream your life away

③ One night the girl had a realistic dream
Her dream world was real, her real world was dream
And down by the river the very next day
She went and she vanished away

④ No one now knows where the sweet girl could be
Though some people say, In the mornings you'll see
Down by the river 'mid castles and jewels
Are maidens and wizards and fools

[C] Now, dream a sweet dream or dream of lust
Dream forever, for dream you must
Or dream a terror and live your dream
And dream your life away

Maidens and Wizards and Fools
3/4 TIME

Ⓥ Verse

D	C	G	A
D	C	G	A
G	A	D	C6+9
C6+9	G	A	D	A

© Chorus

D	C	G	A
Em7	A	D	Bm
G	A	D	C6+9
C6+9	G	A	D	A

Invocation

This multi-part musical chant was first introduced to a large group at the 1989 Merrymeet, Covenant of the Goddess National Meeting. Sung by nearly 200 people, it remains a special moment in my bardic life.

The chant grows as each repeating line of the chorus is built upon the previous one. It builds up to the climax of the invocation verse and gradually grounds itself as the chorus lines withdraw, one by one, til we are left with the original line.

Blessed Be!

Invocation

words and music by Buán The Bard

Invocation

(Chorus)
1. Blessed Be

2. Blessed Be the Gods

3. Ah, Blessed Be the Gods

(Verse)
V. I invoke the Triple Goddess (Goddess)
   I invoke the Horned God (Horned One)
   And together they are the Oneness (Oneness)
   When they join in perfect Love

4/4 TIME

| Em | D | Em | D |

(Repeats)

The polarity of opposites is not magickally a description of difference. Rather, it is an affirmation of the interconnectedness of all things.

Without night, there would be no day. Without either father or mother, there would be no child. Earth and sky interact in harmony and balance. So do such disparate elements as fire and water.

Abstract directions such as left and right, up and down, here and there are all relative to one's perception and perspective.

There is one thing which can encompass all others. It is the idea of a circle.

Blessed Be The Gods

Blessed Be The Gods

words and music by Hugin The Bard

(Instrumental improvisation)

Blessed Be The Gods

① Blessed Be the Gods
　Blessed Be the Gods
　Blessed Be you and I
　Blessed Be earth and sky
　Blessed Be son and daughter
　Blessed Be fire and water

② Blessed Be the Gods
　Blessed Be the Gods
　Blessed Be day and night
　Blessed Be left and right
　Blessed Be up and down
　Blessed Be the circle round

4/4 TIME

D	G	D	D
D	G	D	D
D	D	G	D
D	D	G	A
D	D	G	D
D	D	G	A
D	D	A	D

Three Buckles

The Triple Goddess is most often addressed chronologically youth to age; Maiden, Mother, Crone. The verses of <u>Three Buckles</u> reverse the order.

The subject of the song does dream of the Grandmother, think of the Mother and is with the Lover. These are three manifest aspects of the Triple Goddess.

The object of the chorus is most probably the Grandmother or Crone. She would be more likely to have "hived off" or developed covens under her guidance which had grown up and out to independent existence than would the Lover or even the Mother.

The buckles on the garter represent these covens as badges of adornment and recognition by some Gardnerian groups and others as well.

Three Buckles

words and music by Hugin The Bard

Three Buckles

[C] She was clad in the sky
From her toe to her eye
On her brow
Was a circlet of silver
From her belt, which was blue
Hung a blade, straight and true
On a garter
Three buckles she wore

1. Grandmother, I dream of you still
In the night with the world deep in slumber
I remember the tales you told to us all
And the love that you gave then to me

2. Mother, I think of you still
Though, the world seems a bit torn asunder
I remember the meals you made for us all
And the love that you gave then to me

3. Lover, I am with you still
After what we've been through it's no wonder
I remember the smiles you gave to us all
And the love that you made then with me

[C] She was clad in the sky
From her toe to her eye
On her brow
Was a circlet of silver
From her belt, which was blue
Hung a blade, straight and true
On a garter
Three buckles she wore

Three Buckles
3/4 TIME

C Chorus

D	D7	G	D	
D	D	A	A	
D	D7	G	D	
D	A	G	D	

B Bridge

G	F#m	Bm	G	
D	A	D	A	

V Verse

D	D7	G	D	
D	D	A	A	
D	D7	G	D	
D	A	D	A	

<u>Feather In My Hand</u>

    The Talking Feather is a Native-American invention to help maintain order at meetings or in council. The Holder of the Feather is the one whose turn it is to speak their mind.

    If you find yourself holding the feather, speak honestly what is in your heart, even if you don't understand it. If you are not holding the feather, don't interrupt. This way respect for the sacred and for each other can be maintained and you might learn something.

Feather In My Hand

words and music by Hugin The Bard

Feather In My Hand

① Well, the songs have all grown old
   And the songs have all been new
   You may sing a song I'm told
   But, the song you sing is you

② Well, the world it turns around
   Making circles by and by
   Though a song is more than sound
   And the world is in more than sky

C But, I can't understand
   There's a feather in my hand
   And I can't understand
   Why you do to me
   What you do to me today

③ There is spirit deep inside
   All the things that live
   And throughout the world so wide
   It is love, the song we give

C But, I can't understand
   There's a feather in my hand
   And I can't understand
   Why you do to me
   What you do to me today

Feather In My Hand
4/4 TIME

Ⓥ Verse

E	A	E	E
G	D	E	E
E	A	E	E
G	D	E	E

Ⓒ Chorus

A	E	D	E
A	E	D	D
A	A	E	E

<u>Knights Of The Moon</u>
The distant tromp of boots is heard just moments before the air gently resonates with distant voices singing a marching song. Louder grows the song as the troop emerges from the wood. In raiments of gray and green, brown and blue, they march as if they are all one being.

Their standards are bold. A golden sun, a silver moon, a white wheel of eight spokes on a field of blue and a red star of five points. Here and there are seen bits of trim and weapon tips in silver and bronze. Stag horns and greenery adorn their helms, some of which is in bloom.

The warriors are not segregated by sex. Women and men march together in the ranks. All move with a purpose to their step.

Long after they have marched away and the last of their sounds has faded, the song they sang lingers.

Knights Of The Moon
words and music by Hugin The Bard

Knights Of The Moon

[C] Knights of the Moon, Marching along
Knights of the Moon, Singing her song

(1) For the ladies' love of the Goddess
And the life she nurtures there
For everything on the Earth today
And everything in the air

[C] Knights of the Moon, Marching along
Knights of the Moon, Singing her song

(2) For the Magus of magickal mystery
For the Queen of the whole affair
For the Maiden of motherly magick
And the Wayland who watches there

[C] Knights of the Moon, Marching along
Knights of the Moon, Singing her song

(3) To live our life with the Goddess
And to live it with the Lord
To grow into the Oneness
As the river of life we ford

[C] Knights of the Moon, Marching along
Knights of the Moon, Singing her song

Knights Of The Moon
6/8 TIME

© Chorus

Dm	C	G C	Dm
Dm	C	G C	Dm
Dm	C	G C	Dm
Dm	C	G C	Dm
Dm	D	D

Ⓥ Verse

D	C	G	D
D	C	G	D
D	Dm	Dm

Not surprisingly, <u>Golden Embers</u> was written at a campfire near the meadow of the Fey. It was a sacred fire whose flames leaped and danced and tickled the night air. The fire sang with crackles and pops and the hissing of hot resin from deep within the logs.

Comforting warmth penetrated all who were present. The hypnotic vision of the fire entered eyes and calmed minds and spirits as first the children and then adults drifted off to the land of dreams, til only the Keeper of the Flame remained to watch the golden embers.

Golden Embers

Golden embers and firelight
Hear the song that we sing tonight

Golden embers and firelight
Learn the song that we sing tonight

[C] Sing and rejoice to the song of the fire now
Sing and rejoice to the song of the . . .

Golden embers and firelight
Sing the song that we sing tonight

Golden embers and firelight
Live the song that we sing tonight

[C] Sing and rejoice to the song of the fire now
Sing and rejoice to the song of the . . .

Golden embers and firelight
Hear the song that we sing tonight

Golden Embers
4/4 TIME

Ⓥ **Verse**

| Dm | Dm | C | Dm |
| Dm | Dm | C | Dm |

Ⓑ **Bridge**

| Dm | Dm | C | Dm |
| Dm | Dm | C | Dm |

Ⓒ **Chorus**

| G | Dm | A | Dm |
| G | Dm | A | |

Note: The tenor part of the Bridge follows the Verse melody. The other parts may be added, sung separately, sung in sequence or omitted.

Also, I hold Dm for three extra measures before the Chorus.

The Circle Goes Around

Movement of the four directions anchored to an up and down axis with a central perspective gives gyroscopic balance and stability as the circle goes around.

Within the sacred circle, all things are within all things within the sacred circle. (This is not a typo. Think about it.) Deity is within the people and the people are within Deity as the circle goes around.

Build the song/chant up to singing the five sacred vowel sounds and then descend the way you came. North, east, south, west, up, down, center, the circle goes around.

The Circle Goes Around

words and music by Hugin The Bard

The Circle Goes Around

① North, East, South, West, up, down, center

② The circle goes around

③ The Goddess within me
The God is within me
The Oneness within me
All is within me

④ Ah, Oh, Ooo, Ay, Ee

4/4 TIME

① |D |G A |D |G A |

② |D |G A |D |G A |

③ |D |G A |D |G A |
   |D |G A |D |G A |

④ |D |C G |D |C G |
   |D |C G |D |G A |

Lady Of The Moon

This delightful chant has proved to be both effective and enjoyable. I have used it with and without musical accompaniment to equal effect.

The tune is melodious enough to be called a song rather than a chant and someday it may grow into a full song with verses and chorus.

For the present, I am glad to have a Moon Goddess piece musical enough to draw people in yet simple enough to learn quickly.

Good for raising energy.

Lady Of The Moon

Lady of the Moon
Maiden, Mother, Crone
Granter of the boon
With you we're not alone
We honor you tonight
As we read the rune
Love within your light
Lady of the Moon

4/4 TIME

D	C	G	D
D	C	G	D
D	G	G	D
D	A	A	D

The Mystery

Spiritual seekers of today certainly have their work cut out for them. The day to day mundane world is inundated with materialism. Within those materials seem to be an endless supply of books describing as many different paths to the spirit. There is also no shortage of self-proclaimed teachers calling students to come under their wings. Looking out, it is sometimes difficult to tell the forest from the trees, so to speak.

Well, here's a little secret. The shortest and most direct route to spirit is not out in the world, it is within. All answers of spiritual truth can be found within the sub-conscious, if you know how to get there and where to look.

The only pre-requisites are that you remain vigorously honest to and about yourself and that you maintain an unqualified attitude of love. Otherwise, what you find will not be the truth.

The Mystery

1. I was a seeker, a seeker of light
   I crossed the ocean to see what I might
   Over the ocean and over the sea
   All I could see was me

2. I thought I saw light in the deep sea of blue
   Again when I felt love was coming from you
   There was a calm and there was a gale
   The light was inside of a whale

C. Know ye, know ye the mystery
   Know ye the mystery
   That if that which thou seekest
   Thou findest not within thee
   Thou wilt never find it without

3. Walking the forest and seeking the Crone
   She has the wisdom out living alone
   Then when I saw her, she disappeared
   This had been what I feared

4. Night time above me then I saw the Moon
   I felt my answer would come to me soon
   Reaching for stars, I had missed the mark
   Still stumbling around in the dark
   (Chorus)

5. Seeking for wisdom? It is not a game
   All outside sources can drive you insane
   Then know yourself, if you can abide
   The mystery is always inside
   (Chorus)

The Mystery
3/4 TIME

Ⓥ Verse

Dm	Dm	C	C
F	F	Gm	A
Gm	Gm	F	F
C	C	Dm	Dm

Ⓒ Chorus

Gm	Gm	Dm	Dm
Bb	C	Dm	Dm
C	C	F	F
Gm	Gm	A	A
Bb	C	Dm	Dm

Shenandoah

The old American folk song, Shenandoah, has long been one of my favorites. It's haunting melody and words of love and separation have touched many hearts over the course of generations.

The Shenandoah River divides the Blue Ridge and Appalachian mountain ranges for about 100 miles in northern Virginia and enters the Potomac River at Harpers Ferry. It is very beautiful country. The dictionary attributes the name to the Iroquois language as meaning Spruce Stream.

I have often wondered if the song was originally about the river or a person. In my mind I like to imagine singing this song to an older woman who represents Mother Earth.

Shenandoah (Traditional)

1. Oh, Shenandoah, I long to hear you
   Way Hey, you rollin' river
   Oh, Shenandoah, I long to hear you
   Way Hey, we're bound away
   Cross the wide Missouri

2. Oh, Shenandoah, I love your daughter
   Way Hey, you rollin' river
   Oh, Shenandoah, I love your daughter
   Way Hey, we're bound away
   Cross the wide Missouri

3. Oh, Shenandoah, I'm bound to leave you
   Way Hey, you rollin' river
   Oh, Shenandoah, I'm bound to leave you
   Way Hey, we're bound away
   Cross the wide Missouri

4. Oh, Shenandoah, I long to hear you
   Way Hey, you rollin' river
   Oh, Shenandoah, I long to hear you
   Way Hey, we're bound away
   Cross the wide Missouri

Shenandoah (Traditional)
4/4 TIME — arranged by Hugin The Bard

Ⓥ Verse

D	Bm	F#m	D
G	Em7 A7	D	D△
Bm	F#m	G	G
D	Bm	F#m	G
D	A	D Dsus4	D

Note: I usually substitute D△ for all the D chords. It is presented here as it is, to be easier to play and still sound like the arrangement I have devised.

Reclaimed

These last five songs I wrote several years ago. I have only recently reclaimed them.

In our efforts to reclaim The Goddess as a significant part of our spiritual lives, it is important to first recognize Her in the world around us. Then we can truly begin to express our worship and gratitude for the life, love and beauty She brings to us.

Goddess Delight

words and music by Hugin The Bard

Goddess Delight

1. I wake in the morning and rise from my bed
   Shake out the cobwebs that grew in my head
   I see you in the morning and I see you at night
   I see you in everything, Goddess Delight

2. Thank you for the water I splash on my face
   Thank you for your love for the whole human race
   Thank you for the sunshine and thank you for night
   Thank you for everything, Goddess Delight

3. I see you in flowers and see you in trees
   I see you in birds and in all seven seas
   I see you in the morning and I see you at night
   I see you in everything, Goddess Delight

4. Thank you for the harvest that all of us eat
   Thank you for friends we should happen to meet
   Thank you for the sunshine and thank you for night
   Thank you for everything, Goddess Delight

5. I see you in the animals and in the Earth
   I see you in the heavens and in music's mirth
   I see you in the morning and I see you at night
   I see you in everything, Goddess Delight

6. Thank you for the children that enter our lives
   Thank you for husbands and thank you for wives
   Thank you for the sunshine and thank you for night
   Thank you for everything, Goddess Delight

① At the end of the day as I'm ready to sleep
I pray that my love for you shall ever keep
I see you in the morning and I see you at night
I see you in everything, Goddess Delight

Goddess Delight
3/4 TIME
Ⓥ Verse

E	G#m7	A7	B7
E	G#m7	A7	B7
A7	G#m7	A7	B7
E	G#m7	A7	B7
E	G#m7	A7	B7

Promise Me True

Romantic love has long been an important part of peoples lives. In this song, the story of a romance is portrayed from an ancient perspective.

Back then, people might journey for more than a day to attend High Day festivals. Often lovers would be chosen from within the other community where the traveller may not be well known. Privacy for these liasons would, of course, be preferred.

The practice of privacy and secrecy are part of many magickal and mystery traditions and is reflected in the chorus. Some groups today carry secrecy to the extreme of paranoia. Others seem to exercise it only for the leaders control or punishment of a particular follower. Still, it can not be denied that there have been times when peoples very lives depended upon it.

Promise Me True

words and music by Hugin The Bard

Promise Me True

① Oh, it's greetings my true love away I have been
　Back to my homeland and back to my kin
　Now, let me embrace you and love you today
　If neighbors inquire tho, you know what to say

C Darlin', Don't tell my name
　　　　　　Nor whence I came
　　　　　　That our love remains
　　　　　　Promise me true

② I'll give you a present if I may be bold
　 A candlestick holder of oakwood and gold
　 The gold from an old Viking treasure, now free
　 The wood from the forest of enchanted trees

(Chorus)

③. Oh, give me your sweet lips, I long for them so
　 We've only today, for tomorrow I go
　 Tonight we shall dance and shall sing round the fire
　 May our song reach the heavens, our love send it higher

(Chorus)

④ We met at the Equinox, dancing around
　 And danced at the Solstice, made love on the ground
　 A season I've waited for you in my arms
　 A season of dreaming your bountiful charms

(Chorus)

⑤ In the morning I carry a cauldron away
And travel again for a night and a day
With love in my heart now, this promise I sing
As we danced in the Autumn, we'll dance in the Spring

(Chorus)

Promise Me True
6/8 TIME

Ⓥ Verse

| G | A^m7 | B^m7 | C D |
| G | A^m7 | B^m7 | C D |

Ⓒ Chorus

G F	C	G F	C
A^m7 E^m7	D	D	G
A^m7	B^m7	C D

The Walrus And The Lizard

"The Walrus and the Lizard" is a delightful song with a cast of animals. It was instigated by a spontaneous group of dancing pre-schoolers.

The two main characters are loosely based upon some very loving friends whose nicknames are "Walrus" and "Lizard".

The story line is pure fantasy and not necessarily the story of my good friends.

The Walrus And The Lizard

words and music by Hugin The Bard

The Walrus And The Lizard

C. Oh, the Walrus and the Lizard danced by the sea
   Yes, the Walrus and the Lizard danced so happily

1. But, it wasn't so just a month ago
   When they went to the chapel to be wed
   For that Weasel Preacher said you two are different creatures
   It is sinful that the two of you should bed

2. Then they went into the forest where they shed their tears
   And decided that together they should die
   When the sorry pair spied a Woodland Hare
   Who filled them both with joy with his reply

3. Oh, with all your love, you shall soon be wed
   Seek the Robin, he's a Priestly Bird
   So, now don't be sad, rather do be glad
   He's a right Good Fellow with the word

(Chorus)

4. They were joined together and the scene was grand
   And the cost of the wedding it was free
   By the Giant Oak with the Woodland Folk
   Then the party made it's way down to the sea

(Chorus)

⑤ We will all join hands when the Sun goes down
   We will sing and dance around the fire
   We shall wish them love from the Gods above
   When the Walrus and the Lizard do retire

(Chorus)

The Walrus And The Lizard
4/4 TIME

C Chorus

| D | C | C | D |
| D | C | G | D |

V Verse

G	A	D	D
G	A	D	D
G	A	D	Bm
Em7	G	A	A

Balmy Spring Night

How wonderful it is when Spring warms and brightens our lives and hearts after a long, cold Winter.

Longer days and warmer air allow for evening strolls once more. The smells of Spring growth are, literally, in the air, as those with allergies can attest to.

The Goddess and God are actively engaged in their dance of life which does not take place behind closed doors.

Balmy Spring Night
words and music by Hugin The Bard

'Twas a balmy spring night, I was walkin' with me lover, When much to my delight, We ran into no other, Than the Goddess and the God, Who were walkin' hand in hand, Lovin' on a balmy spring night.

1. Smell the lovely lilac bush, Hail the crimson rose. Gentle breezes kindly push, fragrance up your nose. Life was in the ground, And love was all a-round, On a balmy spring night.

Balmy Spring Night

(C) 'Twas a balmy spring night
　　I was walkin' with me lover
　　When much to my delight
　　We ran into no other
　　Than the Goddess and the God
　　Who were walkin hand in hand
　　Lovin' on a balmy spring night

(1) Smell the lovely lilac bush
　　Hail the crimson rose
　　Gentle breezes kindly push
　　Fragrance up your nose

(Chorus)

(2) Now the nights are growing short
　　Days are growing long
　　'Tis a season made to court
　　How can we go wrong?

(Chorus)

(3) All of life upon the Earth
　　Has a brand new day
　　Going through a new rebirth
　　What more can I say?

(Chorus)

(4) Life was in the ground
　　And love was all around
　　On a balmy spring night

Balmy Spring Night
4/4 TIME

Ⓒ **Chorus**

| G Em | C D | G Em | C D |
| C D | C D | C D | G |

Ⓥ **Verse**

| Bm | Em | Bm | Em |
| A | D | A7 | D |

Ⓑ **Bridge**

| Em Bm | G A7 | C D | G |

Muse Of Mine

There are some who say humans are incapable of creating anything. They claim all creativity is a reflection of the Goddess in our lives. Or, it is the Goddess herself speaking through the individual. In the case of a song, it would be the Goddess in her aspect of the Muse who writes all songs.

I believe the truth of the matter is not a static and definite thing, but is dependent upon one's perspective and perception. I've heard many songs, especially on commercial media, which I'm certain were not divinely inspired. Rather, any loving Goddess might cringe to hear them.

I wrote this song for the creative force in all its loving aspects. A case of creating a song dedicated to that which inspires creation.

"Oh, Muse of mine, you touch my heart."

Muse Of Mine

words and music by Hugin The Bard

Slowly

1. Oh, Muse of mine, you touch my heart, With love's unbound-ed joy. But, lovely Muse, it does confuse me, when you do be coy.

C. Though I am merely mortal, You chose to touch my life, To fill my voice with song and love, nd poetry di-vine.

Muse Of Mine

① Oh, Muse of mine, you touch my heart
With love's unbounded joy
But, lovely Muse, it does confuse me
When you do be coy

② Oh, Muse of mine, you thrill my soul
With magick so sublime
Like this my song, when all along
'Twas you that made this rhyme

© Though, I am merely mortal
You chose to touch my life
To fill my voice with song and love
And poetry divine

③ Oh, Muse of mine, you fill my mind
With mysteries so rare
The magick of the Turtle Dove
And you who're Oh, so fair

④ Oh, Muse of mine, you touch my life
In everything I do
I'll share your love with Gods above
Until this life is through

© Though, I am merely mortal
You chose to touch my life
To fill my voice with song and love
And poetry divine

Muse Of Mine
4/4 Time

Ⓥ Verse

| Dᐃ Em | F#m7 Bm | G Em | F#m7 Bm |

| G Em | D B7 | Em A7 | Dᐃ |

| C G |

Ⓒ Chorus

| G Em | F#m7 Bm | G C | Dᐃ |

| G Em | F#m7 Bm | G A7 | Dᐃ |

| C G |

Merry Meet,
and
Merry Part,
and
Merry Meet
again!

Blessed Be,
Hugin The Bard

On the following page you will find listed, with their current prices, some of the books now available on related subjects. Your book dealer stocks most of these and will stock new titles in the Llewellyn series as they become available. We urge your patronage.

To Get a Free Catalog

You are invited to write for our bi-monthly news magazine/catalog, *Llewellyn's New Worlds of Mind and Spirit*. A sample copy is free, and it will continue coming to you at no cost as long as you are an active mail customer. Or you may subscribe for just $10 in the United States and Canada ($20 overseas, first class mail). Many bookstores also have New Worlds available to their customers. Ask for it.

In New Worlds you will find news and features about new books, tapes and services; announcements of meetings and seminars; helpful articles; author interviews and much more. Write to:

Llewellyn's New Worlds of Mind and Spirit
P.O. Box 64383-K603, St. Paul, MN 55164-0383, U.S.A.

To Order Books and Tapes

If your book store does not carry the titles described on the following pages, you may order them directly from Llewellyn by sending the full price in U.S. funds, plus postage and handling (see below).

Credit Card Orders: VISA, MasterCard, American Express are accepted. Call us toll-free within the United States and Canada at 1-800-THE-MOON.

Special Group Discount: Because there is a great deal of interest in group discussion and study of the subject matter of this book, we offer a 20% quantity discount to group leaders or agents. Our Special Quantity Price for a minimum order of five copies of *A Bard's Book of Pagan Songs* is $59.80 cash-with-order. Include postage and handling charges noted below.

Postage and Handling: Include $4 postage and handling for orders $15 and under; $5 for orders over $15. There are no postage and handling charges for orders over $100. Postage and handling rates are subject to change. We ship UPS whenever possible within the continental United States; delivery is guaranteed. Please provide your street address as UPS does not deliver to P.O. boxes. Orders shipped to Alaska, Hawaii, Canada, Mexico and Puerto Rico will be sent via first class mail. Allow 4-6 weeks for delivery.

International Orders: Airmail—add retail price of each book and $5 for each non-book item (audiotapes, etc.); Surface mail—add $1 per item.

Minnesota residents add 7% sales tax.

Mail orders to:
Llewellyn Worldwide
P.O. Box 64383-K603
St. Paul, MN 55164-0383, U.S.A.

For customer service, call (612) 291-1970.

ANCIENT WAYS
Reclaiming the Pagan Tradition
by Pauline Campanelli, illus. by Dan Campanelli

Ancient Ways is filled with magick and ritual that you can perform every day to capture the spirit of the seasons. It focuses on the celebration of the Sabbats of the Old Religion by giving you practical things to do while anticipating the sabbat rites, and helping you harness the magical energy for weeks afterward. The wealth of seasonal rituals and charms are drawn from ancient sources but are easily performed with materials readily available.

Learn how to look into your previous lives at Yule . . . at Beltane, discover the places where you are most likely to see faeries . . . make special jewelry to wear for your Lammas Celebrations . . . for the special animals in your life, paint a charm of protection at Midsummer.

Most Pagans and Wiccans feel that the Sabbat rituals are all too brief and wish for the magick to linger on. *Ancient Ways* can help you reclaim your own traditions and heighten the feeling of magick.

0-87542-090-7, 256 pgs., 7 x 10, illus., softcover $14.95

CELTIC MYTH & MAGIC
Harness the Power of the Gods & Goddesses
by Edain McCoy

Tap into the mythic power of the Celtic goddesses, gods, heroes and heroines to aid your spiritual quests and magickal goals. *Celtic Myth & Magic* explains how to use creative ritual and pathworking to align yourself with the energy of these archetypes, whose potent images live deep within your psyche.

Celtic Myth & Magic begins with an overview of 49 different types of Celtic Paganism followed today, then gives specific instructions for evoking and invoking the energy of the Celtic pantheon to channel it toward magickal and spiritual goals and into esbat, sabbat and life transition rituals. Three detailed pathworking texts will take you on an inner journey where you'll join forces with the archetypal images of Cuchulain, Queen Maeve and Merlin the Magician to bring their energies directly into your life. The last half of the book clearly details the energies of over 300 Celtic deities and mythic figures so you can evoke or invoke the appropriate deity to attain a specific goal.

This inspiring, well-researched book will help solitary Pagans who seek to expand the boundaries of their practice to form working partnerships with the divine.

1-56718-661-0, 464 pgs., 7 x 10, illus., softcover $19.95

LIVING WICCA
A Further Guide for the Solitary Practitioner
Scott Cunningham

Living Wicca is the long-awaited sequel to Scott Cunningham's wildly successful *Wicca: A Guide for the Solitary Practitioner.* This new book is for those who have made the conscious decision to bring their Wiccan spirituality into their everyday lives. It provides solitary practitioners with the tools and added insights that will enable them to blaze their own spiritual paths—to become their own high priests and priestesses.

Living Wicca takes a philosophical look at the questions, practices, and differences within Witchcraft. It covers the various tools of learning available to the practitioner, the importance of secrecy in one's practice, guidelines to performing ritual when ill, magical names, initiation, and the Mysteries. It discusses the benefits of daily prayer and meditation, making offerings to the gods, how to develop a prayerful attitude, and how to perform Wiccan rites when away from home or in emergency situations.

Unlike any other book on the subject, *Living Wicca* is a step-by-step guide to creating your own Wiccan tradition and personal vision of the gods, designing your personal ritual and symbols, developing your own book of shadows, and truly living your Craft.

0-87542-184-9, 208 pgs., 6 x 9, illus., softcover $12.95